Mid-Hudson Memories

A photographic retrospective of the 1940s - 1960s

Acknowledgments

"Mid-Hudson Memories: A Photographic Retrospective" resulted from the coordination of many who lent specific expertise in several areas.

The book would not have been possible without the institutional knowledge of John R. Flanagan, a retired Poughkeepsie Journal copy editor who spent nearly 40 years at the newspaper. John's encyclopedic expertise of the Journal's 70 years of archives, as well as his memories of Dutchess County and the mid-Hudson Valley, proved to be invaluable resources during photo selection, fact-checking and proofing. John spent dozens of hours going through photo envelopes and files that had not been opened, in some cases, in 60 years. His numerous recommendations about how to best provide a full pictorial look at the 1940s-1960s, and his guardianship and love of history, are appreciated by all at the newspaper.

Executive Editor Stuart Shinske coordinated the book's content. Senior Local Editor John Ferro provided thorough copy editing. Data Desk Editor Ray Fashona wrote the introductions to each chapter, creating an overview and context on each of the three decades profiled. Nancy Haggerty, a freelance contributor to the Journal, wrote the photo captions with creative flair. Market Development Manager Jean Harris coordinated promotion of the book.

A huge debt of thanks goes to mid-Hudson Valley residents who searched through photo albums, scrapbooks, attics, basements and closets to offer the Journal treasured images of a bygone era. The public's enthusiasm for this project is greatly appreciated by the Poughkeepsie Journal's staff. This book is for you – and everyone who holds Dutchess County in his or her heart.

Enjoy.

Barry Rothfeld
president and publisher
Poughkeepsie Journal and PoughkeepsieJournal.com

Copyright© 2008 • ISBN: 978-1-59725-163-1
All rights reserved. No part of this book may be reproduced, stored in a retrieval system or transmitted in any form or by any means, electronic, mechanical, photocopying, recording or otherwise, without prior written permission of the copyright owner or the publisher.
Published by Pediment Publishing, a division of The Pediment Group, Inc. www.pediment.com Printed in Canada

Foreword

Welcome to "Mid-Hudson Memories: A Photographic Retrospective."

The allure of today's mid-Hudson Valley emanates from its rich history, scenic beauty and its inspirational residents, past and present.

Since Aug. 11, 1785, the Poughkeepsie Journal and its forerunners have chronicled the region's special quality of life. This is an area that spawned innovations that revolutionized, without a doubt, the nation. And the 1940s through the 1960s were critical years in powering that impressive evolution.

The world's largest computer company, IBM, has employed tens of thousands here who provided the brainpower behind technological advancement that continues today.

Prominent residents such as Franklin and Eleanor Roosevelt guided history via their actions, standards and concern for their fellow Dutchess County residents – even during a world war that was managed, in part, from historic Hyde Park.

And the millions of others who called this region home in those 30 years provided their own contributions, large and small, noticed and unnoticed, that created the fabric for the mid-Hudson Valley we know today.

Our region is a beautiful, lush area that is a magnet for the creative. For the contemplative. And as much as the valley has given to us, its residents have given back to the valley.

This book is dedicated to everyone who loves Dutchess County and the mid-Hudson. The photos in the following pages depict what drives that special feeling – then, now and in the future.

We hope you enjoy this trip back in time. Thank you for reading.

Barry Rothfeld
president and publisher
Poughkeepsie Journal and PoughkeepsieJournal.com

Note: Photo caption information was based on information in the Journal's archives or what was provided by readers who submitted the image.

Table of Contents

The 1940s: War, IBM, the Baby Boom 7

The 1950s: Prosperity, Communism, Idealism 59

The 1960s: JFK, The Counterculture, Suburbia 95

The 1940s: War, IBM, the Baby Boom

The 1940s began as a time of uncertainty. But as 1949 turned into 1950, the foundation for generations of prosperity in the mid-Hudson Valley would be set.

With the dawn of 1940 came hope for an end to the economic suffering created by the Great Depression. But the nation, and Dutchess County, were wary. In Europe, war was growing more severe. Adolf Hitler had seized Poland in 1939, and by June 1940, Germany controlled much of Europe, including France. While some Americans saw the United States' intervention as inevitable, others insisted on a continued policy of isolationism, spawned by World War I.

Everything changed after Dec. 7, 1941, when Japanese planes devastated Pearl Harbor. America, led by President Franklin D. Roosevelt of Hyde Park, was thrust into war. The economy gained full traction as the country ramped up its military might. In the valley, young men left their homes and jobs to go into battle. In many instances, they were replaced by women who took manufacturing and other jobs traditionally held by men. Factories kept humming; the machine of war kept cranking.

World War II dominated the first half of the decade. However, Roosevelt didn't live to see the Allied Forces' victory. The nation's longest-serving chief executive died of a cerebral hemorrhage in Warm Springs, Ga., in April 1945 at the age of 63. Weeks later, Germany would fall, and in August, Japan surrendered after President Truman ordered atomic bombs dropped on Hiroshima and Nagasaki.

With the war over, men returned to their jobs and families. Many women left the workplace -- but they had tasted independence and there was no going back. The seeds for the women's and civil rights movements had been planted.

Dutchess County, like much of America, experienced a post-war growth spurt. More people bought homes thanks to the booming economy and mortgages underwritten by the federal government. Large estates began to give way to suburban housing developments. Workers commuting to their jobs meant skyrocketing car sales and road improvements, a trend that would eventually turn South Road into the multi-lane Route 9.

Dutchess' biggest economic news of the 1940s came in 1948, when IBM dedicated its sprawling Poughkeepsie plant, serving 3,000 employees. For the first time, thanks to the GI Bill, many attended college, an option that had been out of reach for some. The decade ended with a baby boom and a more educated workforce, setting the stage for compelling local and national change.

LEFT: In a massive patriotic showing, Arlington school students join an estimated 7,000 marchers as they make their way past more than 20,000 people May 17, 1942, in Poughkeepsie during the "I am an American" Day parade. *Courtesy Poughkeepsie Journal archives*

RIGHT: No cell phones, no push-button phones and, for him, not even a rotary dial. Still, James Van Tassell, 90, communicated just fine with a customer while taking an order in December 1940 at his general store near Clinton Corners. The store opened in 1810. *Courtesy Poughkeepsie Journal archives*

BELOW: He might have dropped the title fight to him twice but here in November 1940, Melio Bettina (right) stands tall with world light heavyweight champion Billy Conn. The two men and state Boxing Commissioner Bill Brown (center) watched amateur boxers this day at the Wappingers Falls Central School gymnasium. *Courtesy Poughkeepsie Journal archives*

BOTTOM LEFT: New leaders emerge at Amenia High School in October 1940, with the election of senior class officers: Richard Foley, vice president; Janet Thompson, president; Anna Downey, secretary; and Edmund Thomassen, treasurer. *Courtesy Poughkeepsie Journal archives*

BELOW: Today it might be much more expensive, but this 1941 model fit the Poughkeepsie Fire Department's budget in November 1940. Standing by his new ride is Fire Chief Chris W. Noll. *Courtesy Poughkeepsie Journal archives*

ABOVE: With peace soon to end for the United States, local sailors Ralph M. Horrocks and Harold Kipp of Hyde Park and Robert Flannery and Samuel Mirto of Poughkeepsie spend part of their October 1940 leave from the Naval Training Station in Newport, Rhode Island, locally with Chief Machinists Mate Honin L. Dehart and Chief Boatswain's Mate John McGuire of the area's recruiting station. *Courtesy Poughkeepsie Journal archives*

ABOVE: Ushering in a new year of government at Millerton High School in October 1940 are (left to right) newly elected Senior Class President Donald Mathews, advisor Jeanette Rother, Vice President Margaret Schlichting, Secretary Matilda Passini and Treasurer Helen Van De Bogart. *Courtesy Poughkeepsie Journal archives*

RIGHT: A snowplow works to unearth landing strips at the Dutchess County Airport after a heavy January 1948 snowfall. *Courtesy Poughkeepsie Journal archives*

TOP RIGHT: Directors of the first swimming meet held at Spratt Park Pool pose in August 1940. They are (front row, left to right) James Corcoran, Charles Haight and Dick Key and (back row, left to right) Al Marino, John Devorscik, John Hannan, Cynthia Nickerson, Irene Siko, Kathleen Rappelyea, Samuel J. Kalloch, Earl Brower, Alice Whitesell, Ken Zimmer, Dorothy Campitelli and Richard M'Cabe. *Courtesy Poughkeepsie Journal archives*

ABOVE: Things cost just a bit less in the 1940s, including this new snowplow, which cost LaGrange $9,500. *Courtesy Poughkeepsie Journal archives*

LEFT: Hats may have been the order of the day but how often did Eleanor Roosevelt follow convention? Here, the former first lady hosts members of Dutchess County's Democratic women's clubs at a garden party and tea at her Val-Kill home in Hyde Park. *Courtesy Poughkeepsie Journal archives*

BELOW: Skirts didn't stop anyone from climbing fences and traversing fields to follow beagles tracking a hare during a three-day event in Millbrook in October 1940. *Courtesy Poughkeepsie Journal archives*

ABOVE: It wasn't square to square-dance in the '40s, at least not in Clinton Corners, where radio and movie star Lanny Ross (center) paired with Mrs. C. Allerton Morey. Ross and his wife are buried in Union Vale. *Courtesy Poughkeepsie Journal archives*

BELOW: It might be the British countryside but, in fact, this October 1940 hunt is beginning in Beacon. The sponsor was the Rombout Hunt Club. *Courtesy Poughkeepsie Journal archives*

ABOVE LEFT: A merry Christmas is anticipated by Poughkeepsie Fire Chief Chris W. Noll, who sits among some of the refurbished toys that were given in 1940 to an estimated 1,500 poor children in the city. The toys were collected by police and firefighters. *Courtesy Poughkeepsie Journal archives*

ABOVE RIGHT: There can be little doubt who employs these delivery boys, who were rewarded with a trip to New York City after increasing their deliveries, circa 1940. Front row, from left, William Miller, Russell Granter, Herbert Hawkes and Kenneth Miller. Back row is unidentified. *Courtesy Poughkeepsie Journal archives*

BELOW: A train crossing the railroad bridge over the Hudson River, circa 1940. *Courtesy Robert Auchincloss*

TOP: Tom Thumb's wedding is celebrated here among Wappingers Falls Central School kindergarteners in June 1940. Front row, left, three unknown girls, Joseph Garnot, Barbara Lahey, Bobbie Di Santis and Richard Drake. Back row, left to right, Barbara Helding, Relande Morgan, Barbara Lupperalo, Jean M'Kinney, Mary M'Nerney, Marlene Repecki, John Foster, Donald Smith and Bobbie Dolan. *Courtesy Poughkeepsie Journal archives*

ABOVE: A ticket to gain entrance to the bridge to watch the Intercollegiate Regatta, Poughkeepsie, June 18, 1940. *Courtesy Marion (D'Luhosch) Ceiles*

LEFT: Poughkeepsie Journal building in the process of being built in 1940.
Courtesy Poughkeepsie Journal archives

OPPOSITE: Armistice Day 1940 is celebrated in Poughkeepsie with a parade.
Courtesy Poughkeepsie Journal archives

BELOW: The Rutherford House, a Poughkeepsie landmark located at 85 South Hamilton Street, was purchased on August 22, 1940 by Mr. George E. and Marion S. Rutherford for their dance studio, which is still in operation, and their home. The house is now owned by their daugher, Barbara Ann Rutherford. Prior to the Rutherford ownership, in the 1960s the house was built and owned by Captain John H. Brinkerhoff to look like his ferry boats that he operated between Poughkeepsie and Highland. Brinkerhoff was also captain of the "Mary Powell."
Courtesy Barbara Rutherford

BOTTOM LEFT: Boy Scouts and officials attended the outdoor Boy Scout court of honor of the Greater Poughkeepsie area at College Hill. Front row, from left, Donald Crooks, R. J. Horn, Lewis Tompkins, Walter Whippo, sea scout; Arthur Rowe, Pleasant Valley; George Balassone, John Brophy. Second row, Henry Klump, Dennis Crooks, Bernard Luchton, George Wilkinson, Jr., Jacob Holzwarth, Jr., Charles Tompkins, William Dragstra. Third row, James Dow, standing holding flag; Kermit Borst, George Davis, Jr., Ronald Tice, William Freer, Edward Moshier, holding flag. Back row, City Judge Benjamin Roosa, Beacon; Walter C. Forse, scout executive; Justice of Peace Carlton B. Fitchett, Paul Samuels, area commissioner. *Courtesy George T. Wilkinson*

ABOVE: Vassar and Dartmouth students enjoy a day on the Hudson near Hyde Park in May 1940. From left are Margery Gerdes, Malcolm Smith, Jim Wilbee, Alan Priddy and Helen Ebeling. *Courtesy Poughkeepsie Journal archives*

BELOW: Wappingers Central School, Route 9, 1940. *Courtesy Timothy P. Holls*

ABOVE: Group outside of the Beacon Laundry building, built in 1929. Photo, circa 1940. Those known are Tom Malloy, Edna Best Gilbandt, Emil Baer, Urbino "Worby" Ciancanelli, Libby Orr, Lois Tomlins, Sarah Ritter (holding Leo Ritter) and Joseph Ritter. *Courtesy Helen Ritter and Frank Ritter Studio*

RIGHT: Albert Schottler, Jr. of Wappingers Falls sits in his 1909 Ford during a sunny July day in 1941. *Courtesy Poughkeepsie Journal archives*

BELOW: The man regarded as one of the world's all-time greatest athletes—track, football and baseball star Jim Thorpe (second from left)—sits with Dutchess County Judge J. Gordon Flannery (l), Frank L. Gardner, Sr. and Dean H. Temple at a Poughkeepsie YMCA dinner in February 1941. Thorpe was the dinner's guest speaker. *Courtesy Poughkeepsie Journal archives*

ABOVE: Swimming at the beach at Norrie Playground on the Hudson River in Staatsburg, circa 1940. *Courtesy Judy Linville*

RIGHT: On patrol in what was then called a "prowl" car, Poughkeepsie Police Sergeant Frank J. McManus uses the department's new two-way radio system to call headquarters in May 1941. *Courtesy Poughkeepsie Journal archives*

OPPOSITE: It wasn't exactly today's Long Island Expressway, but traffic is still a nuisance in August 1941 on Manchester Road, which had just become the new link between Poughkeepsie and the Taconic State Parkway. *Courtesy Poughkeepsie Journal archives*

ABOVE: Robert Schaefer, driving in a 1929 Dodge Touring Car that was cut down to make a haywagon, Pleasant Valley, circa 1941. *Courtesy Denise Byrnes*

RIGHT: Members of the Harlem Valley basketball team, wearing knee pads of the era, pose in February 1941. Front row, left to right, John Gilbert, Steve Gilbert, Ken Ritchel and John (Skip) Rucinski. Back row, left to right, Joe Duffy, Buddy Finn, Phil Ruggiero and Jack Lyons. *Courtesy Poughkeepsie Journal archives*

FAR RIGHT: Poughkeepsie High School guidance and personnel service department members Robert Ross, Ann Neuwirth and Lubin Anderson at work in January 1941. *Courtesy Poughkeepsie Journal archives*

TOP RIGHT: A flurry of potential shoppers descend on the remodeled Perlmutter Furniture store on Main Street in Poughkeepsie in October 1941. Police had to provide crowd control as an estimated 15,000 people attended this open house. *Courtesy Poughkeepsie Journal archives*

ABOVE: The Amenia Town Hall and Fire Department building stands destroyed following a December 1941 fire. *Courtesy Poughkeepsie Journal archives*

LEFT: The Millbrook Giants, 1940-41. Top row, from left, Monroe Bennett, Walter "Toot" Patrice, Al Potter, Chick Cornelius, Sonny Bradford, Cliff West, Cliff West, Jr., Preston Bennett, Jim Gordon, Ernie Duncan, Sr. (owner and manager). Second row, John Qualls, Ross Reed, Austin "Audie" Bennett, Chet Nicholas, Morg Reed, Jules Wood, Bob Magill. Front row, Ernie Duncan, Jr. and Leroy Reed. *Courtesy Walter Patrice*

TOP LEFT: My Own Brucie, the cocker spaniel, was top dog in many ways. Here, the two-time Westminster Kennel Club champion poses in 1941 after one of those victories. Left is Brucie's owner/handler, Herman Mellenthin of Poughkeepsie. Center is show chairman Jay Gould Remick. At right is Judge Joseph Sims. Brucie, who was honored with a testimonial dinner in Poughkeepsie, was a nationally known pooch, who, among other things, helped sell U.S. war bonds. *Courtesy Poughkeepsie Journal archives*

ABOVE: The Poughkeepsie basketball team, sponsored by the Brown Derby, January 31, 1941. Edmund Sokol, is pictured, bottom right. He donated this photograph and was 90 years old in the summer of 2008.
Courtesy Edmund Sokol

LEFT: The eighth-grade class of Warring School on Mansion and Smith streets, 1941. First row, sitting on ground: Richard W. Oestrike, Lionel Bolin, Jimmy Barden, Fred Wilser, Herbie May, William Doughty, Gerald Fay, Billy Chamuras. Second row, Betty Gallagher, Shirley Speedling, Shirley Polokoff and Barbara Gibson. Third row are Alvin Perlmutter, Florence Steinberg and Billy Kustas, holding the flag. The others are unidentified. *Courtesy Richard W. Oestrike*

BOTTOM LEFT: Where did famed actress Gloria Swanson make her stage debut? On the Arlington High School stage during a production of "Reflected Glory" in late June 1942. Swanson, center, is greeted at the Poughkeepsie Train Station by Mrs. Robert Callender, left, chairwoman of the performance benefiting the Poughkeepsie Junior League and Kiwanis Club, and John Wallberg, right, the Kiwanis president. *Courtesy Poughkeepsie Journal archives*

BELOW: Feeding his pig and, in turn, the war effort in August 1942 is Poughkeepsie resident Ernest Hatfield. Hatfield told the Poughkeepsie New Yorker (now the Poughkeepsie Journal) that his decision to focus on farm work and not actively campaign for the GOP State Assembly nomination saved tires and gasoline, both in short supply at that time. The decision didn't seem to hurt Hatfield, a 10-year city alderman, who served in the Assembly for five years before putting in another 17 in the state Senate. He retired in 1964 and died in 1977 at age 86. *Courtesy Poughkeepsie Journal archives*

BELOW: Members of the Catharine Street Community Center gather for a June 1942 father-son dinner. Left to right, are John W. Harden, Robert Magill, Director Frank T. Wood Jr., Board of Directors Chairman Dr. R. W. Morgan, the Reverend Arthur E. May of AME Zion Church and Louis H. Key. *Courtesy Poughkeepsie Journal archives*

BOTTOM LEFT: Campers from the Jewish Community Center prepare to leave for Camp Brandeis in July 1942. Front row, left to right, are Judy Cohen, Debra Rosenstein, Lorraine Postoff, Barbara Bloom, Marilyn Hyman, Betty Cohen and David Goler. Middle row, left to right, Donald Spitz, Deborah Bergman, Irma Sachs, Stanley Newman, Marion Dinerstein, Joan Lazark, Myra Bernzweig, Laura Goler, Elaine Segel and Shirley Rubin. Back row, left to right, are camp director Eli Kogos and counselors Grace Cohen and Sholom Kahn. *Courtesy Poughkeepsie Journal archives*

ABOVE: Barbara Hammond (Beckett) and Jeanne Hammond at their family farm, circa 1942. *Courtesy Jeanne H. Byrnes*

OPPOSITE: Many of America's baseball heroes were off to war. But back home, life went on in July 1942 as a new generation of players took to the diamonds. Here, at the Pittsburgh Pirate-run American Legion baseball school at Riverview Field (now Fred Stitzel Field) in Poughkeepsie, Pirate coach and scout Fred (King) Lear (right) talks about pitching with hurler Bob (Two Gun) Cady of Arlington (left). Looking on are, left to right, Howie Williamson of Millbrook, Bob (Jolly) Tompkins of Amenia, Joe Fulton of Wappingers Falls, Stan Bloomer of Arlington, Jack Brophy of Poughkeepsie and Bill Allen of Rhinebeck. *Courtesy Poughkeepsie Journal archives*

BELOW: Aerial view of Greenvale Riding Academy, Poughkeepsie. The Vassar College girls boarded their horses here. *Courtesy Coleen and Dan McCarthy*

RIGHT: New Union College graduate Raymond E. Aldrich, Jr. of Poughkeepsie sits with Wendell L. Willkie moments before commencement exercises in May 1942. Willkie, the honorary chancellor of Union who lost the 1940 presidential election to Franklin Roosevelt, gave the principal address and received an honorary degree. Aldrich had impersonated Willkie in a gridiron skit earlier in 1942. *Courtesy Poughkeepsie Journal archives*

BOTTOM RIGHT: Rose Capano (bottom), Theodore Lovelace, and Louise Lovelace at a swimming hole, summer of 1942. *Courtesy Julie Lovelace Barilics*

BELOW: Workers at Schatz Federal Bearings assemble airplane bearings as part of the war effort in July 1942. The plant employed more than 400 women at the time. *Courtesy Poughkeepsie Journal archives*

ABOVE LEFT: The government needed rubber and in 1942, Blackie's, a Clinton Square shop, was more than willing to help out. Here, employee Alfred Benack stands by a pile of used tires that was expected to yield 4,000 pounds of rubber. *Courtesy Poughkeepsie Journal archives*

ABOVE RIGHT: Elmer Gunce Brown in front of his home on 10 Spring Street, Wappingers Falls, 1942. *Courtesy Karen L. Hallock*

LEFT: Vince McDowell, Bob Coughlin, Hugh McDowell, Harry Plimly and George Robillard, 1942. *Courtesy Ann Coughlin*

ABOVE: Trying to spark interest in the Community War Chest, local Boy Scouts hold cards in 1942, showing the names of organizations that will benefit from the local drive. In the front row, left to right, are John Van De Water, John Pemberton, Edmund Dubois, George Harjes, Charles Nejame, Robert Snyder and Linford Snyder. Middle row, left to right, Edgar Raymond, Robert Secor, Roger Vandemark, Gerald Voerman, Charles O'Donnell and Carleton C. Kirchner. Top row, left to right, Albert Drake, Margaret A. Ryan, Mrs. Harry D. Matteson, William Moehrke, Edmond J. Reuter, Doran Paul O. Sullivan, Rabbi Jerome Unger and John J. Kuhn. *Courtesy Poughkeepsie Journal archives*

ABOVE: The Dutchess County Pistol Association grew in popularity during World War II, when it held nightly practice and instruction. From left to right in February 1942 are William Olah, Rudy Eisert, Einar Reeves, club secretary Al Greco, Stanley Post and Frank McManus. *Courtesy Poughkeepsie Journal archives*

RIGHT: Keeping an ear for enemy activity in June 1942 are Pleasant Valley Aircraft Listening Post daytime workers Mrs. Kenneth D. Sherow and Mrs. Allen V. Sherow, who flank chief observer Louis B. Hajos. More than 200 people, including high school students, took turns manning the post, which operated 24 hours a day. *Courtesy Poughkeepsie Journal archives*

BOTTOM RIGHT: Millbrook basketball team, 1942. Included in the photo are Charles Johnson, Chick Cornelius, Don Willis, Oscar Boone, Don Hollman, Ernie Duncan, Jr., Julius Wood, Erwin Jackson, Walter Patrice and Coach Ernie Duncan, Sr. *Courtesy Walter Patrice*

BELOW: Ellsworth Bay Bohlinger, Jr. was a signalman, first class, aboard the U.S.S. Indianapolis, which served in the Pacific circa 1942. *Courtesy Cindy Cameron*

ABOVE: Volumes of water are sprayed into the Hudson River in October 1943, as the Poughkeepsie Fire Department demonstrates new pumpers it obtained through the Office of Civilian Defense.
Courtesy Poughkeepsie Journal archives

ABOVE: Planting seeds of patriotism, children tend to one of the 65 Victory Gardens they planted with the support of the Poughkeepsie Garden Club. *Courtesy Poughkeepsie Journal archives*

LEFT TOP: Bob Coughlin, Army Air Corps. pilot, 1943. Coughlin was a bombardier pilot. *Courtesy Ann Coughlin*

LEFT BOTTOM: Dominic Gallo, a volunteer for the Army Air Corps ground crew, just before leaving for the war, December, 1943. *Courtesy Angelina Gallo*

RIGHT: Joseph C. Domin was a dairy farmer in LaGrange, 1943. *Courtesy Jo Ann Wright*

FAR LEFT: Louis (Butch) Delsanto sitting in a flower pot at 142 North Hamilton Street, Poughkeepsie, 1943. *Courtesy Marylou Sotanski*

LEFT: Mae and Lee Boice pick up spilled coffee during the war years because rationing was in effect, 1940s. *Courtesy Pam and Gary Veeder*

BOTTOM: Ice, created by water from fire hoses, covers the Hotel Windsor in Poughkeepsie following a February 1943 fire. *Courtesy Chris Weisner*

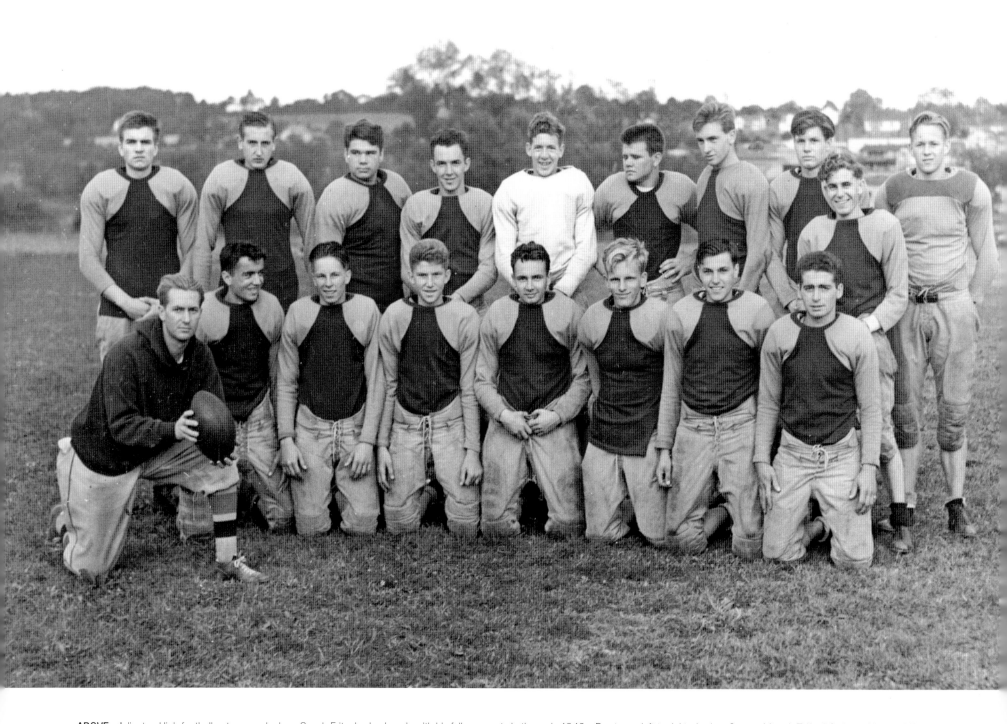

ABOVE: Arlington High football gets a new look as Coach Fritz Jordan kneels with his fall prospects in the early 1940s. Front row, left to right, Jordan, George Murad, Telford Graham, Vincent D'Angelo, Joseph Elton, Robert Laird, William Whitely and Tony D'Angelo. Back row, left to right, Jake Holzwarth, Creighton Schroeder, Wallace Stevenson, Burr Powell, Ben Ross, Harold M'Issac, Albert Mulford, Ray Pascoe, Marvin Murphy and Robert McAllister. *Courtesy Poughkeepsie Journal archives*

ABOVE: Playmates pose near Gasparro's Bakery on Mill Street in Poughkeepsie, circa 1944. Girls from left are Joanne Aliotta, Sylvia DeFidi and Jacke Aliotta. The boy is Horatio DeFidi. *Courtesy Joanne Aliotta Drivas*

LEFT: Mike Casement and Pam Boice and their mud pies at South Grand Avenue in the 1940s. *Courtesy Pam and Gary Veeder*

TOP LEFT: From left, Willard Schultz, Grace Robertson, and Neil K. Robertson on a Hudson River Day Line boat in the summer of 1944. *Courtesy Grace R. Chartier*

BOTTOM LEFT: F. Messarad, William Stafford, William Callahan and Fred Robinson outside of Beacon Dutchess Tools on July 22, 1944. *Courtesy Patricia Way*

FOLLOWING LEFT: Celebrating military victory in Europe, more than 5,000 people pack Poughkeepsie's Market Street May 8, 1945. The Poughkeepsie High School band performed. *Courtesy Poughkeepsie Journal archives*

FOLLOWING TOP RIGHT: Circa 1945, from left, Mrs. Smith Johnson, broadcaster Lowell Thomas, Dr. Norman Vincent Peale and Smith Johnson. Smith Johnson was the founder of the Pawling Rubber Company in Pawling. *Courtesy Stanley E. Woron*

FOLLOWING BOTTOM RIGHT: The S.S. Vassar, named to honor Vassar College, cuts through Chesapeake Bay May 24, 1945, during her maiden voyage. The ship, which was earlier christened by Vassar Student Government President Elizabeth Gatchell, was assigned to transport cargo and soldiers. *Courtesy Poughkeepsie Journal archives*

RIGHT: Joshua "Jot" Turner (1865-1957) in the shop of The New York State Department of Transportation. He was a sign painter for Pawling Company. Photo, circa 1945. *Courtesy Stanley E. Woron*

OPPOSITE: Merrymakers descend on downtown Poughkeepsie August 14, 1945, to celebrate the Japanese surrender marking the end of World War II. An estimated 50,000 celebrated into the next day on Main Street and the surrounding business district. *Courtesy Poughkeepsie Journal archives*

BELOW: An empty 200-pound safe is brought to shore at the Hudson's Whitehead sand dock in August 1946. The safe was apparently dumped in the river after being stolen. Pictured are (left to right) Dutchess County Sheriff's Deputies Albert Von Duisburg, Larry Quinlan and Robin Adams, and Sheriff C. Fred Close. *Courtesy Poughkeepsie Journal archives*

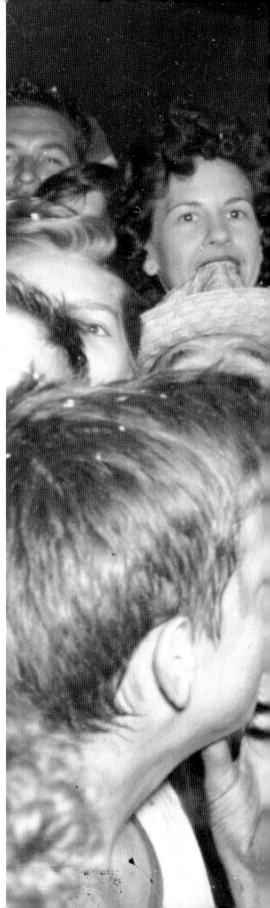

ABOVE: Maura Rowe and David Smith lay a wreath on President Roosevelt's grave on Memorial Day in Hyde Park, 1945. *Courtesy Margaret Golnek*

TOP LEFT: Local cadets from St. Francis Hospital's School of Nursing prepare to leave for six months of training at England General Hospital in Atlantic City. Front row, from left, are Poughkeepsie's Grace Kearney, Mary Eileen Walsh and Sarah Filoia and Marlboro's Dorothy M'Court. Middle row, left to right, are Croton-on-Hudson's Joan Grant, Marlboro's Joan Morehead, Poughkeepsie's Johanna Niet and Rhinebeck's Gloria Wheeler. Back row, left to right, are Garfield, New Jersey's Eleanor Kasica and Pleasant Valley's Mildred Ruehle. *Courtesy Poughkeepsie Journal archives*

BOTTOM LEFT: Jumping is Homer Grey, master of the hunt, Greenvale Farms, 1940s. *Courtesy Coleen and Dan McCarthy*

OPPOSITE: A good used car costs more today, but in the 1940s, $7,395 was enough for Poughkeepsie to purchase this snowloader, which is put to use here for the first time following a January 1942 snowfall. *Courtesy Poughkeepsie Journal archives*

ABOVE: Roe Movers was established by Floyd C. Roe, far left, in the early 1920s to haul goods back and forth across the Hudson River using the ferry. Mr. Roe's two sons, Floyd and Leslie, are pictured to the far right. This picture was taken in front of the old Western Publishing Company, circa 1945. Though Roe Movers was sold in the mid 1960s, the Roe name is retained by the current company.
Courtesy Linda Roe MacIssac

RIGHT: Tom Curatolo snapped this photo of a passenger train with "Poughkeepsie" stamped on the side while stationed in Japan with the U.S. Army, 1945.
Courtesy Tom Curatolo

FAR RIGHT: View of the Pawling Rubber Company, Pawling, circa 1945. The company is still in business today. *Courtesy Stanley E. Woron*

LEFT: Eighth-grade graduation of Krieger School on South Grand Avenue, 1945. First row, from left, Elizabeth Kallock, Joan Gray, Margaret Dietrick, Raymond Crodelle, Lawrence Stamm, James Effron, Patricia Laffey, Raymond Lindholm, Everett Rood, Joan Mae Wanders, Patricia McManus and Anita Smith. Second row, Terry Rawson, Arthur Rideout, James Carlon, Shiela Whalen (Somen), Rosemarie Becchetti, Margaret (Peggy) Gardner (Larkin), Ruth Spiers, Jane Spross, Robert Kozlark, Douglas Robertson and David Beatty. Back row, Mrs. Stone, Robert Long, Raymond Mallhouse, Jane Heaton, Sally VanNosdall, Catherine McCourt (Michel), Victor Davis (principal), Martha Prenting, Nancy Kutz (O'Shea), Joan Idema, Charles Russell, Gordon Rogers and Miss S. Kelly. *Courtesy Catherine (McCourt) Michel*

BELOW: The Hudson River Day Line Dock in Poughkeepsie, where boys would routinely get dayliner passengers to throw coins to them. The boys would dive in to retrieve the coins and stuff them in their cheeks. Photo, circa 1945 *Courtesy Joe Vitelli*

ABOVE: A group celebrates Al "Chick" Cecchini's 22nd birthday at the home of Mr. and Mrs. Alfred Cecchini, Sr. on Kelsey Road in Poughkeepsie, 1946. To celebrate the birthday, Al and his friends dressed up in their uniforms. Front row, seated are Howard Knauss, Gerry Scott and Bill Fichtell. Seated in back are Mal Kilmer, Truman "Bab" Armstrong, Bill Scott, Burt Whitaker, George Lozier, Alec "Sandy" Anderson, Howie North and Terry Barr. *Courtesy Burt Whitaker*

RIGHT: Santa delivers presents in December 1946 to the 82 children living in the Children's Home in Fairview. The party, which included a dinner and entertainment, was put on by Victory Lodge No. 1598 of the International Association of Machinists. Here, party chairman Edwin Terpening (back) helps distribute the gifts. *Courtesy Poughkeepsie Journal archives*

LEFT: Joseph P. Mansfield Sr. and Marion D. Robinson Mansfield together, 1947. Joseph was home on leave because their daughter Kathleen had been born. *Courtesy Joe Mansfield*

FAR LEFT: A century of service is celebrated January 22, 1947, as the Poughkeepsie Children's Home marks its 100th anniversary. Here, children from the home look on as Mrs. T.V.K. Swift, a former Home Board of Managers president, cuts the cake. Joining them are (left to right) former board presidents Mrs. E. Sterling Carter and Mrs. Robert Burr and then-current board president Mrs. John Wilkie. *Courtesy Poughkeepsie Journal archives*

ABOVE: A champion for a day, Briarcliff Laddie No. 1 poses with owner Betty Pottenburgh, 16, of Rhinebeck after winning the 4-H baby beef title at the Dutchess Fair in August 1946. The celebration was sadly short-lived for the 1,015-pound Aberdeen Angus, who was immediately auctioned off to Gallagher's Steak House in New York City at $1.25 a pound. *Courtesy Poughkeepsie Journal archives*

ABOVE: Toasts abound at the American Legion's Lafayette Post on Mill Street among crew members of the USS Darby, who were on hand October 28, 1946 to help celebrate Poughkeepsie's Navy Day.

Courtesy Poughkeepsie Journal archives

ABOVE: Wappingers High School students treat their foreign exchange students with a trip to Val-Kill. Eleanor Roosevelt is in the middle with the family dog, Fala. Teacher and advisor to the students (standing, top left) is Dennis Hannah; to his left is Bob Piggott, standing directly behind Mrs. Roosevelt. Photo, 1947. *Courtesy Mark F. Piggott*

BELOW: Jack Garno dressed as a Native American for a parade at Clinton Square in Poughkeepsie, 1947. *Courtesy James Metrando*

BELOW: The big man in town March 4, 1947, is none other than former heavyweight boxing champ Primo Carnera, who dwarfs George Palmateer, then-sports editor of the Poughkeepsie New Yorker, now the Poughkeepsie Journal. Carnera wrestled in Newburgh the day before, winning his match in 12 minutes. *Courtesy Poughkeepsie Journal archives*

ABOVE: The Sunday comics have enthralled kids (and adults, for that matter) for generations. Here, in 1948 in Poughkeepsie, twins James (left) and Robert (right) Blanchard look at them with sisters Caroline and Patricia.
Courtesy Poughkeepsie Journal archives

ABOVE: William J. Long riggers move a large section of plating equipment at IBM in Poughkeepsie, 1947. Pictured is a 1926 Mack Truck. William J. Long was a local company from 1918 to 1981. *Courtesy John K. Long*

RIGHT: Members of the Krieger Elementary School Chronicle have reason to write about themselves in 1948, as they captured the Superior Award given by the Columbia Scholastic Press Association. Seated left to right are David Flinchbaugh, typist; Dorothy Ackerman, assistant editor; Patricia Underhill, editor-in-chief; and Ellen Chuck of the art department. Standing left to right are Constance Rawson and Janet Storm of the business department and Toby Devan, assistant editor. *Courtesy Poughkeepsie Journal archives*

BELOW: Locomotive at the Poughkeepsie train station, circa 1947. *Courtesy David and Kathleen Ferris*

ABOVE & BELOW: Dorchester Arms Motel, Route 9, 1960s. This is the current location of Circuit City, Poughkeepsie. *Courtesy Timothy P. Holls*

RIGHT: Tivoli High School students work on their art projects in the home of Tivoli artist George Englert in February 1948. The art class was offered to select students. Sitting left to right are Peter Sturges, Sanford Moore and Kenneth Neal. Standing are (left to right) Larry Takacs, Florence Dowdell, Florence Lester and Michael Teck. *Courtesy Poughkeepsie Journal archives*

BELOW: Running off their dinners beforehand, contestants take off at the start of the annual YMCA Thanksgiving 10-mile race in Poughkeepsie November 25, 1948. Left to right is eventual winner William Steiner of the Bronx; Bill Clark, John Neupauer, Paul Sadowski and Bernie Hemmindinger, all of the Jersey Athletic Club; John Sullivan and John Berthelot of the Milrose Athletic Association; Stanley Johnson of Princeton; Carmon Phillips of Highland, who was running for Milrose; and Herbert Benario, Mike O'Hara, Barry Murphy and Martin I. Shepard, all of the New York Pioneer Club. *Courtesy Poughkeepsie Journal archives*

LEFT: Robert Schaefer and Irene Mattiasich Schaefer stand by a 1930 Model A Ford they drove to California for their honeymoon. Photo, 1948. *Courtesy Denise Byrnes*

FAR LEFT: The big name locally in amateur sports in 1948 was Ray Billows. Here in February 1949, Billows, the 1948 Metropolitan Amateur golf champion and runner-up in the National Amateur Championship, accepts the Poughkeepsie New Yorker Trophy from sports editor George Palmateer, right, after readers voted him the area's top amateur athlete. The New Yorker is currently known as the Poughkeepsie Journal. *Courtesy Poughkeepsie Journal archives*

BELOW: Gentlemen start your.... OK, there are no engines in Soap Box Derby racing, but there's still plenty of speed. Here, five competitors line up on Poughkeepsie's Academy Street hill to test their cars in preparation for the July 1948 city derby. Left to right are Leaonard Kent, Malcolm Delamater, Richard Hall, Fred Wohlfahrt and Joseph Bogart Jr. The actual race was staged on Brickyard Hill. *Courtesy Poughkeepsie Journal archives*

RIGHT: The waters are warm and inviting in August of 1949 at Sprout Lake for New York City kids with cardiac disorders. These children, chosen by city clinic doctors and social workers, enjoyed four weeks of camp at Sprout Lake. *Courtesy Poughkeepsie Journal archives*

OPPOSITE: It isn't quite an Indy car but this soapbox racer was still pretty fast as it captured the Poughkeepsie Soapbox Derby to qualify for the August 1949 Soapbox Derby Nationals in Ohio. Here, winning driver Bobby McCord, 13, and his mother, Stella, look on as Bobby's dad, Chester E. McCord, and brother, Chester R. McCord, carefully load the racer for transport to the Nationals. *Courtesy Poughkeepsie Journal archives*

BELOW: Before he appeared in one of history's most infamous headlines, "Dewey Defeats Truman," New York Governor Thomas E. Dewey and his wife are welcomed in Pawling in June 1948 after he won the Republican nomination for president. *Courtesy Poughkeepsie Journal archives*

RIGHT: Future fun is on the horizon in June of 1949 as Catharine Street Community Center Board Chairman Mrs. John R. Jackson cuts the ribbon opening a new playground area at the community center. Looking on are (front row, left to right) Dolores Jackson, Elizabeth Wells and Shirley Lee Roberts and (back row, left to right) Friends of the Center President Mrs. Harold R. Dean, Center Director Frank T. Wood, Jr., Board Vice President Reverend Charles E. Byrd, Edward Presler and James Reed. *Courtesy Poughkeepsie Journal archives*

BELOW: The Andrews family leaving for a camping trip at Lake George, July 1949. Family members are Jeff Andrews (father), Agnes (mother) and children Mae, Jim and Tom. The truck is a 1929 Model A Ford. Photo taken on Columbia Street in Poughkeepsie. *Courtesy Jim Andrews*

BOTTOM: John D. King, salesman for Diesing Supply Company, Poughkeepsie, 1949. *Courtesy Roger J. Diesing*

ABOVE: Arthy Denning and the Blue Jays Football Team, circa 1949. *Courtesy John M. Canning*

RIGHT: Opening more of Dutchess and points north to further development, Governor Thomas E. Dewey, a Pawling resident, applies a torch to a chain at a new section of the Taconic State Parkway in Freedom Plains. Attending the October 1949 ceremony were (left) Francis R. Masters, chairman of the Taconic State Park Commission, and (right) Robert Moses, state Council of Parks Chairman. *Courtesy Poughkeepsie Journal archives*

BELOW: Flying high in July 1949, members of the Poughkeepsie Civil Air Patrol are congratulated by Lieutenant Commander Joseph Crowley after passing inspection at their headquarters at Dutchess County Airport in New Hackensack. From left are Lieutenant Kenneth Dean, Crowley, Lieutenant Donald Kehn and Lieutenant James Liffert. *Courtesy Poughkeepsie Journal archives*

ABOVE: Catherine and Barbara McCourt dressed in their Easter outfits to visit their aunt Teshia Flanagan in Beacon, 1949. *Courtesy Catherine (McCourt) Michel*

ABOVE: Frank Ritter and his father, Louis Ritter, at 81 South Hamilton Street, circa 1949. *Courtesy Helen Ritter and Frank Ritter Studio*

OPPOSITE: At left, Pat Keenan and Joey Healy at the Hopeland Rest Camp in 1949. The camp was founded by Harry St. John Cooke in 1924 and was just east of Fishkill. The others in the photo are unidentified. *Courtesy Patrick and Dorris Manning*

BELOW: George Luesing at a pharmacy in Poughkeepsie, 1949. *Courtesy Helen Osterhoudt*

ABOVE: Fishkill may be known today for stores and traffic but the story was a bit different in August 1949. Here, Alexander MacTavish flies low to dust a bean field on Blodgett Farm. *Courtesy Poughkeepsie Journal archives*

BELOW: Stormville celebrates the laying of the cornerstone on a new firehouse in October 1949. Poughkeepsie Deputy fire Chief Frank Gardner (seated second from right) served as dedication speaker. *Courtesy Poughkeepsie Journal archives*

The 1950s: Prosperity, Communism, Idealism

The 1950s dawned with optimism. The American economy was healthier than it had been in 30 years as consumers bought houses, cars and televisions at a record pace. As IBM flourished, Dutchess County continued to grow. Construction of Route 9, started at the end of 1949, was completed, easing transportation from south to north. Meanwhile, cities like Poughkeepsie began a long, slow decline as the middle class fled for the manicured lawns of suburbia.

Shopping malls also started to pop up, drawing retail traffic out of once-busy urban areas. The Poughkeepsie Plaza opened on Route 9 in the Town of Poughkeepsie in November 1958, starting a frenzy of commercial growth along the corridor that continues today.

Despite its chrome exterior, the 1950s were not as utopian as they appeared. Americans felt threatened by the world's other superpower, the Soviet Union, which had tested its first atomic weapon in 1949. Communism was perceived as a tangible threat, and the "red menace" led to the rise of power of U.S. Sen. Joseph McCarthy, the Wisconsin Republican who interrogated, often unjustly, many Americans to identify alleged traitors. Among those questioned: Dutchess County's own Pete Seeger, a folk singer and peace advocate.

The struggle between capitalism and communism sparked the Korean War in 1950 as the United States and its allies battled China and the Soviets for control of the peninsula. The war ended in 1953 with a divided Korea and more than 33,000 dead American soldiers.

Pivotal developments in the growing civil-rights movement occurred as well. In 1954, the segregation of black and white students in schools was ruled unconstitutional. A year later, a black woman named Rosa Parks refused to give up her bus seat to a white man. Her arrest sparked a bus boycott in Montgomery, Ala., that incited a violent reaction against its main organizer, Dr. Martin Luther King Jr.

Elected in 1952, low-key President Dwight D. Eisenhower endures as a symbol of the 1950s, but he was to be succeeded by a vibrant young president named John F. Kennedy. The conservative 1950s were about to explode into the turbulent, memorable 1960s.

LEFT: Violet Elementary School teacher Penelope Svendsen looks on as Delores Corey, Thomas McCormack and Jay Eitzen play their violins in February 1950. *Courtesy Poughkeepsie Journal archives*

ABOVE: Twelfth Night carolers sing and an accordionist plays by a giant Christmas tree-fueled bonfire in January 1950 during a ceremony sponsored by the Junior Chamber of Commerce and Poughkeepsie Recreation Commission at Memorial Field.
Courtesy Poughkeepsie Journal archives

TOP LEFT: Salt Point farmer Louis Fish, Jr. (second from right), the new chairman of the Dutchess 4-H, talks about cows in January 1950 during a visit to a neighbor's farm. Left to right, are his daughter, Karlene; a neighboring Holstein; Johanne Hahn, Raymond Olson, Barbara Hahn and Jeanne Hahn.
Courtesy Poughkeepsie Journal archives

BOTTOM LEFT: Hooked on industrial arts or at least fishing, Arlington High students craft their own fishing rods in March 1950. Instructor John J. Stewart (center) talks about one rod with student Walter Seaboldt. Other students pictured are (left to right) Donald Cary, William Doelling and Harland Metcalf.
Courtesy Poughkeepsie Journal archives

OPPOSITE: Mardi Gras in Poughkeepsie? Yes, and not a small celebration either. Here, part of an estimated crowd of 60,000 watches as high school students "row" the Junior Chamber of Commerce float during the 1950 celebration.
Courtesy Poughkeepsie Journal archives

RIGHT: Caruso farm, off Route 9G between Poughkeepsie and Hyde Park, 1950. Family members would travel from Yonkers in a truck to spend the weekend at the farm. On the left is Rose Moltari and Concetta Caruso, center. *Courtesy Nancy Cirone*

FAR RIGHT: George Kaplan (left) and Keene Simmons (right) pose prior to their June 1950 boxing match in Poughkeepsie. Kaplan won in a unanimous eight-round decision. *Courtesy Poughkeepsie Journal archives*

BELOW: New York Giants catcher Wes Westrum (front right/center) congratulates John Avello (front left/center) after Avello, the manager of the Schatz team, was named the Twilight League's Manager of the Year in 1950 at the league's annual dinner in Poughkeepsie. Left to right behind them are playoff MVP Jimmy Gordon; League President John Babiarz; regular season MVP Ken Prince; Chicago White Sox farmhand Carl "Jake" Charter; former New York Yankee first baseman Dick Kryhoski, Austin Knickerbocker, an outfielder with Baltimore of the International League; and Mickey Witek, former Giant and Yankee infielder. *Courtesy Poughkeepsie Journal archives*

ABOVE: Gene Autry, on horse to the right, visits Poughkeepsie during the 1950s. *Courtesy William J. Brill*

BELOW: Francis Cardinal Spellman, archbishop of New York and president of the St. Francis Hospital Board of Trustees, helps lay the cornerstone of the more than $2 million Oakleigh Thorne and Joseph E. Tower memorial wings on May 24, 1950. *Courtesy Poughkeepsie Journal archives*

ABOVE: Martha and Lawrence Graham, owners of Graham's Florists, 1950. The business was open from 1914 to 1969. *Courtesy Evelyn Tario*

BELOW: One of the many parades held on Main Street in Poughkeepsie during the 1950s. *Courtesy William J. Brill*

ABOVE: Thanksgiving Day Parade in Poughkeepsie, circa 1950. *Courtesy Jo Ann Wright*

RIGHT: John Bocchino, one of the head gardeners at College Hill Royal Cemetery, circa 1950. *Courtesy Matilda Mastrocio*

TOP: Ralph and Charlie (standing in doorway) Morano operated this service station in Wappingers Falls during the early 1950s. *Courtesy Valli Morano*

OPPOSITE: In August 1950, when New York City was rich with baseball, these boys were rewarded with a trip to see the Giants play the Dodgers after winning Poughkeepsie's Derby Playground Junior and Midget League championships. Here, they wait to board the bus to the game as league director Sam J. Kalloch checks them in. *Courtesy Poughkeepsie Journal archives*

ABOVE: The Alexander Hamilton docking on the Hudson River for a day of shopping in Poughkeepsie, circa 1950.
Courtesy William J. Brill

RIGHT: Charlie Secore, proud owner of a new Studebaker, Wappingers Falls, 1950.
Courtesy Jane Edgar Secore

FAR RIGHT: Dutchess County Airport, circa 1950.
Courtesy George Macy

LEFT: Workers at IBM in Poughkeepsie, 1950. From left, Albert Bohlinger, George Bohlinger, Ellsworth Bohlinger, Sr., Ellsworth Bohlinger, Jr. and Harold Bohlinger. *Courtesy Helen Osterhoudt*

BOTTOM LEFT: Mechanics from Poughkeepsie's Western Publishing (printer of Golden Books and Dell Comics) with fleet of trucks, circa 1950. From left, John Trethewey, Charles Steiner and Walter Johnson. *Courtesy Carol Trethewey Beck*

BOTTOM MIDDLE: Earl Armstrong at Dongan Square on Mill Street, Poughkeepsie, in the fall of 1950. *Courtesy Patty Sacerdote*

BELOW: Al Miller, Dolores Armstrong, Bertha Miller, Mary Miller and Fran Miller stop for a family photo at Dongan Sqaure on Mill Street, Poughkeepsie, 1950. *Courtesy Patty Sacerdote*

ABOVE: Adding a touch of Hollywood glamour to the event, actor, producer/director Robert Montgomery (center) appears at the May 1951 Dutchess County American Red Cross dinner at Nelson House in Poughkeepsie. Left is dinner vice chairman Charles H. Adler. Right is dinner chairman F. Paul Deuell. Montgomery, who died in 1981, was no stranger to the area. He grew up in Beacon and owned a home and shooting preserve in Millbrook for 25 years. *Courtesy Poughkeepsie Journal archives*

LEFT: Finding some pleasure in a war zone, Corporal James Kalliche of Poughkeepsie, center, listens as Corporal Elmas E. Sweet of Kentucky plays an organ discarded by Communist forces in Korea in the spring of 1951. *Courtesy Poughkeepsie Journal archives*

OPPOSITE: Mechanics from Western Printing (printer of Golden Books and Dell Comics) with a fleet of trucks, circa 1950. From left, Walter Johnson, Floyd Moffit, Ralph Conklin (in front), Louis Muraso, Charles Steiner, John Trethewey and Harold Sutherland. *Courtesy Carol Trethewey Beck*

LEFT: Poughkeepsie firefighters battle a three-alarm blaze in a Catharine Street apartment building in March 1951. No one was injured but nine families were left homeless. *Courtesy Poughkeepsie Journal archives*

BELOW: Poughkeepsie was still somewhat rural and harness racing was still hugely popular in 1951, when Thomas W. Murphy drove Kimberly Kid around his training track off Hooker Avenue. Murphy, who sold Kimberly Kid for $150,000 in 1955, was a renowned breeder and trainer who won the famed Hambletonian in 1956 with The Intruder. Murphy, whose horses set numerous world records, was inducted into the Harness Racing Hall of Fame. He died in 1967.
Courtesy Poughkeepsie Journal archives

ABOVE: View of upper Main Street, looking west toward the river, Poughkeepsie, June 15, 1951. *Courtesy Joanne Aliotta Drivas*

OPPOSITE BOTTOM LEFT: Wedding day of Edward P. Ringwood and Margaret F. Murphy on September 9, 1951. They were married at St. Peter's Church on Mill Street in Poughkeepsie.
Courtesy Kathleen M. M. Ringwood-Wood

OPPOSITE MIDDLE: Charles Secore and Jane Edgar before heading out to the Arlington High School senior prom, 1951. *Courtesy Jane Edgar Secore*

OPPOSITE BOTTOM RIGHT: Flames gut a barn after it was apparently struck by lightning at Vassar College in Poughkeepsie in August 1951. A campus garage also was destroyed.
Courtesy Poughkeepsie Journal archives

ABOVE: Annual Sheldon Drive Fourth of July parade, 1952. This event began during World War II when gas rationing eliminated driving to downtown Poughkeepsie to watch the parade. Grace Chartier of Red Oaks Mill is the tall girl in the center of the photo. *Courtesy Grace R. Chartier*

BELOW: Before hitting the water, candidates for the 1952 Poughkeepsie High crew team work out indoors as coach Joe Ryan looks on. Front to back are Don Grimm, Mario Scalzi, Joe Wallwork and Bob McCord. *Courtesy Poughkeepsie Journal archives*

ABOVE: St Peter's sixth-grade class, 1951. *Courtesy John M. Canning*

BELOW: Hyde Park's first ambulance, 1952. From left are Harold Farley, David Ray, Clayton Ray (driver), and Alfred Overfield. This 1952 Packard was donated by the Morris Cantor car dealership in 1952. *Courtesy Patrick M. Ray*

ABOVE: Cheerleaders from Poughkeepsie High School gather for a team shot on College Hill in 1952. The cheerleaders cheered the football team onto the championship in the DUSO League that year. Also significant about this squad was that Dorothy "Dot" McGue (pictured second from left) was the first African American cheerleader at the high school. From left, Sally Blazejewski, Dot McGue, Phyllis Satz, Shirley Van Nosdall, Dot Ackerman, Debby Spoor, Tillie Betz, Pat Kenney, Terry Acker and Marilyn Chick. Absent from the team photo were Kippy Pleninger, Joan Stanley and Annaliese Meixner. *Courtesy Dorothy E. McGue Didymus*

ABOVE: Girl Scout Troop 15 has its picture taken at the Dutch Reformed Church in the early 1950s. *Courtesy Pam and Gary Veeder*

BELOW: Paul Kefor's deli at the corner of Mansion and Washington streets, Poughkeepsie, 1950s. *Courtesy Paul Kefor*

ABOVE: Robert W. Monell, employee of Baxter's Pharmacy on Water Street in Newburgh, collecting money for the American Cancer Society, 1952. Monell later owned and operated Monell's Camera Shop in Newburgh for more than 40 years. *Courtesy Cathy Coppinger*

BELOW: Robert and David Ferris playing checkers, Poughkeepsie, 1954. *Courtesy David and Kathleen Ferris*

TOP LEFT: William Sift sitting on the porch of a large rooming house at 13 South Grand Avenue, Poughkeepsie, 1954. *Courtesy Irene Barbuto*

TOP MIDDLE: Garrett and Ferris Garage, owned and operated by Ed Garrett, Robert "Pete" Ferris and Carlos Campbell, 1954. The business was on Dutchess Turnpike in Poughkeepsie. *Courtesy David and Kathleen Ferris*

TOP RIGHT: Richard Joseph Hirmberger down the road from his country family summer retreat and from his great-grandfather's house, which was also the residence of his parents. Photo taken near the Fish Creek wood bridge on Fish Creek Road, Saugerties, 1953. *Courtesy Richard Joseph Hirmberger*

BELOW: Large rooming house (bed and breakfast) at 13 South Grand Avenue in Poughkeepsie, 1954. *Courtesy Irene Barbuto*

ABOVE: Eleanor Roosevelt was the guest speaker for commencement at Oakwood Friends School in June 1954. She is shown with William Clark, principal, Jerome Hurd, president of the board of managers, and Ruth Craig, long-time teacher and assistant principal. Founded in 1796, Oakwood Friends School is New York State's oldest co-educational boarding and day school. It is an independent, college preparatory school serving grades 6-12. *Courtesy Kathy Moyer*

ABOVE: Cleaning up after August 1955 flooding, members of the Salt Point Fire Department pump out the basement of a Pleasant Valley home. *Courtesy Poughkeepsie Journal archives*

BELOW: Who were the fastest coon dogs in the country in 1957? That was determined at the American Grand National, held in Hyde Park, where multiple dogs hit an amazing 35 miles per hour. Pictured here at the Crum Elbow Sportsmen's Association are (left to right) Cliff Crowell of Maine with Morning Star; field judge Bill Shorty; Denny Forehouse of Syracuse with Black Powder; and P.J. Clark of Massachusetts with overall winner Sailor. *Courtesy Poughkeepsie Journal archives*

ABOVE: Siblings Marla and Tom Kefor, Fishkill, 1955. *Courtesy Marla Hill*

BELOW: The Hudson still occasionally freezes over but it was a much more common occurrence years ago. Here, the chill of late January 1955 in Poughkeepsie is evident. *Courtesy Poughkeepsie Journal archives*

ABOVE: A 4-H parade in front of Diesing Supply Company, circa 1955. *Courtesy Roger J. Diesing*

LEFT: Marjorie Campbell arrived home from Washington, D.C. to a crowd of hundreds of Red Hook residents at the Barrytown Railroad Station after she won first place at the national cherry pie contest on February 23, 1955. Pictured here are her two sisters Barbara and Carole, her mother and father, Ingeborg and Richard Campbell Jr., and her grandfather Richard Campbell Sr.
Courtesy Marjorie Campbell Fountain

BELOW: View looking north from Main Street Bridge in Wappingers Falls during the 1955 flood.
Courtesy Village of Wappingers Falls

OPPOSITE: YMCA Y-Teens Club members Sheila Bilyou and Jacqueline Smith receive instructions at the Dutchess County Health Association on how to fill kits to be used by volunteer workers at the February 1957 Heart Sunday event. *Courtesy Poughkeepsie Journal archives*

RIGHT: Robert W. Monell and Jean Marie Lynch engagement photo in 1956, Newburgh.
Courtesy Cathy Coppinger

ABOVE: Sophomores hold a chain of daisies to honor Vassar College's Class of 1958. Two-hundred and ninety-nine women graduated that year. *Courtesy Poughkeepsie Journal archives*

OPPOSITE: Training to help police with rescue work and more, members of the Dutchess Divers join Trooper Paul Paquet (left front) at the Hudson in August 1956. Kneeling in the front are (left to right) Joseph Gleason and Richard Lott. Standing, left to right, are Irving Hoffman, Andrew Hartzell, Martin Compasso, William McGaugrin, Alfred Thomas and Lewis Pasch. *Courtesy Poughkeepsie Journal archives*

ABOVE: Linda Lovelace (Mack) and sister Donna Lovelace (Mierzwa) at their first communion celebration, May 1956. *Courtesy Julie Lovelace Barilics*

ABOVE: Construction of the education wing at First Baptist Church at 260 Mill Street, Poughkeepsie, 1957. *Courtesy Grace R. Chartier*

BELOW: Cardinal Farley Military Academy graduation, 1957. Cadet Major John K. Long, Sr. graduated with his class in 1957. The academy was a private school in Rhinecliff on the Levi P. Morton Estate from 1945 until 1965. *Courtesy John K. Long*

ABOVE: The Wappinger Creek can hardly even qualify as a mudhole in July 1957, the result of a long, region-wide drought. *Courtesy Poughkeepsie Journal archives*

BELOW: Allan C. Masch and Chris Masch on a 1949 Harley Davidson in front of the family-owned kennels on Old Post Road in Wappingers Falls, 1957. *Courtesy Tom Masch*

TOP: Kathy and Jo Ann Domin dressed up in their Easter dresses made by their mother, Barbara Domin in 1957. *Courtesy Jo Ann Wright*

ABOVE: Front office of Emery & Webb, Inc., circa 1955. Employees Helen Day, at the left rear, Louisa Burks, center rear; owner Henry Emery, right rear, employee Louis Schiller, center and an unknown person in the front. *Courtesy Tom Sipos, Emery & Webb*

RIGHT: Notre Dame football hero and Poughkeepsie resident Monty Stickles is toasted with a parade down Main Street in December 1958. *Courtesy Poughkeepsie Journal archives*

ABOVE: Thanksgiving dinner at the Monell family home. From left are Debbie, Hazel, Curt Sr. (holding Cathy), Helen, Curt, Jean, Marjorie and Jeri (in high chair), November 28, 1957. *Courtesy Cathy Coppinger*

OPPOSITE: In 1958, a new concept emerged — education via television. (Left to right) Morse School first-graders Konrad Edwards, Gregory Capen and Pauline Bartel tune in to New York educational channel WPIX. At the time, four Poughkeepsie schools were taking part in the program. *Courtesy Poughkeepsie Journal archives*

LEFT: Kids enjoy a miniature train during Staatsburg Community Day celebrations, June 1955. *Courtesy Margaret Golnek*

BELOW: With a snip, a new era begins as 13-year-old Nancy Ruth Heppner opens the Kingston-Rhinecliff Bridge in February 1957. Watching are (left) her father, Ernest, Kingston's member on the New York Bridge Authority; and (right) Governor W. Averell Harriman. *Courtesy Poughkeepsie Journal archives*

RIGHT: Father Peter Cody of St. Peter's Church with Joseph P. Mansfield Jr., 1958. *Courtesy Joe Mansfield*

FAR RIGHT: Murray A. Perlman takes a break to catch his breath at a family picnic and hiking trip in the Minnewaska area, 1958. *Courtesy Carolyn VanBrookhoren and Judith Perlman*

BELOW: Service men at Wright & Wright garage, a Nash Rambler dealership on the Dutchess Turnpike, Poughkeepsie, 1958. *Courtesy David and Kathleen Ferris*

ABOVE: Stock car racing, circa 1958. *Courtesy Jim Banks*

LEFT: Cathy Monell on Christmas Day in 1958. *Courtesy Cathy Coppinger*

FAR LEFT: Original Byrnes Message Bureau switchboard, Poughkeepsie, circa 1958. *Courtesy Denise Byrnes*

RIGHT: The Cold War was raging but thawed a little for at least one day as Soviet Premier Nikita Khruschev (right) and his wife join Eleanor Roosevelt, center, in Hyde Park in September 1959. Khruschev placed a wreath on the late president's grave. Background left is Soviet Foreign Minister Andrei Gromyko. *Courtesy Poughkeepsie Journal archives*

BOTTOM LEFT: Marking the 350th anniversary of the discoveries of both the Hudson River and Lake Champlain, State Senator Ernest I. Hatfield (right) and state engineer Kurt G. Rauer unveil a marker in Millerton, near the Connecticut line, in August 1959. *Courtesy Poughkeepsie Journal archives*

BOTTOM MIDDLE: Former U.S. Open golf champion Gene Sarazen takes a look at tractors at the 1959 Dutchess County Fair in Rhinebeck. Sarazen owned a farm in Columbia County. *Courtesy Poughkeepsie Journal archives*

BOTTOM RIGHT: When flannel uniforms were king, one of the local princes of baseball was Poughkeepsie's Billy Ostrom. The lefty swinging Ostrom, shown here in 1959, starred in the Colonial and Twilight leagues for Poughkeepsie teams in the '40s and '50s. He also played in the Interstate League into the '60s and was a youth coach. *Courtesy Poughkeepsie Journal archives*

ABOVE: Lifeguard Austin Bentley shows off a handstand on top of a Chevy at Travis Picnic and Swimming Grove on Sprout Creek in LaGrange, circa 1959. In the background, swimmers wait to use the diving board. Holiday weekends would bring 300 or more people to the popular recreation spot. *Courtesy Austin Bentley*

LEFT: Lonnie Fishman and Norman Gershon, first cousins, at Awosting Falls, 1959. Lonnie lived with his mother Cele (Fishman) Steinberg and sister Gladys (Fishman) Gottlieb at 199 Main Street. Cele was a secretary at The State University at New Paltz Admissions Office for many years. *Courtesy Carolyn VanBrookhoren and Judith Perlman*

BELOW: It's the end of the line in October 1959 for these manually operated railroad gates in Barrytown. The last of their type in Dutchess County, they were soon replaced by automatic, electric gates. *Courtesy Poughkeepsie Journal archives*

ABOVE: The last students to attend the 160-year-old, one-room Little Red Schoolhouse on Red School House Road, Fishkill, 1959. *Courtesy Joan Smith*

LEFT: Mary Osterhoudt and Dale Sherman and friends at the swimming pool in the park across from Joe's Pizza stand in Lincoln Center, 1959. *Courtesy Dale Sherman*

OPPOSITE: A Coast Guard cutter breaks ice by the Mid-Hudson Bridge in Poughkeepsie in February 1959.
Courtesy Poughkeepsie Journal archives

The 1960s: JFK, The Counterculture, Suburbia

The social and cultural upheaval that defined the 1960s had been fermenting for two decades. Blacks and women, empowered by their roles in World War II, sought equal status. An unpopular war in Vietnam, which would take the lives of 58,000 American troops, gave young people a focus for their disillusionment with authority. Protests erupted in the mid-Hudson Valley and throughout the country, with the counterculture's signatures being drugs, long hair and rock music.

In 1963, President Kennedy, whose election in 1960 as a young, charismatic figure fueled American idealism, was assassinated. Five years later, his brother, U.S. Sen. Robert Kennedy, was slain while making a run for president. Civil rights leader Martin Luther King Jr. was gunned down the same year.

The valley played a prominent part on the turbulent stage of the 1960s. A report in the Aug. 18, 1963 Poughkeepsie Journal noted that more than 200 area residents left Poughkeepsie "at 3 a.m. today to participate in the March on Washington, D.C. They traveled aboard five chartered buses that started from Ebenezer Baptist Church, Smith Street and Winnikee Avenue."

Another symbol of the counterculture, LSD guru Timothy Leary, took up residence in Millbrook from 1962 to 1968. He was visited by the likes of William Burroughs and Jack Kerouac. The defining event of the movement, the Woodstock Music and Art Fair in August 1969, happened in the Sullivan County town of Bethel. Many local residents remember how the flood of traffic heading toward the historic concert closed down highways.

Back in Dutchess, the county's continuing growth led to the establishment of the first county executive position in 1967. David C. Schoentag of Beekman was elected to the post. IBM's international success spurred expansion locally, as Big Blue opened a 100,000-square-foot manufacturing facility in East Fishkill to complement its Town of Poughkeepsie operations. And Vassar College, for more than a century an elite higher education institution for women, went co-ed in 1969.

Through it all, the mid-Hudson Valley's intrinsic attractions – natural beauty, history and quality of life – sustained and evolved, solidifying the region as a top place to live in the nation.

LEFT: Clifford M. Buck (right) of Salt Point, a guide with the Pomona Grange, talks about cow farming at Harold E. Miller's Hereford spread in Dover in July 1963. Left is Stephen Krom, 14, with Robert Gilbert Jr., 13. The Hyde Park boys visited the farm as part of a Town/Country Days tour. *Courtesy Poughkeepsie Journal archives*

RIGHT: Hudson Valley teens and adults listen to Pete Seeger give a concert at Beacon High School, Nov. 28, 1965.
Courtesy Poughkeepsie Journal archives

ABOVE: Brewing up support for their candidate, in August 1960, former First Lady Eleanor Roosevelt (left) of Hyde Park hosts the first of a planned 100 coffees for 29th Congressional District candidate Gore Vidal (right). Mrs. Carl Silber of the Town of Poughkeepsie (center) was district coordinator of what was billed as "Coffee Hours for Vidal." *Courtesy Poughkeepsie Journal archives*

BELOW: New York Governor Nelson Rockefeller, who in the next decade would become vice president of the United States following President Nixon's resignation, here campaigns for Nixon in October 1960 in Beacon, while also attending "waterbreaking" ceremonies for the new Newburgh-Beacon Bridge. Behind him are (left to right) Hudson resident Dr. John L. Edwards, chairman of the State Bridge Authority, and authority member Benjamin J. Slutsky of Ellenville. *Courtesy Poughkeepsie Journal archives*

ABOVE: Looking more like spacemen than anything else, Poughkeepsie Fire Lieutenant Chocianowski (left) and Fairview Captain Jack Whalen (right) walk over burning boards and hot coals near the Fairview firehouse to test new fire suits in June 1960.
Courtesy Poughkeepsie Journal archives

LEFT: Mose Van Benschoten, racer at Arlington Speedway, Poughkeepsie, 1960. *Courtesy David and Kathleen Ferris*

BOTTOM LEFT: Bud Marl, racer, at Arlington Speedway, 1960. *Courtesy David and Kathleen Ferris*

BOTTOM RIGHT: Hardy Parker, Sr. and Lula Mae Parker with their children Renee, Hardy, Jr. and Monique Parker, 1960. They were on Christmas holiday at the home of their grandparents, Frank and Easter Parker, at 195 Smith Street. *Courtesy Lula Mae Parker Harris*

BELOW: Colonel Henry Ludington's Mill in Kent, Putnam County shortly before it burned in 1966. *Courtesy Stanley E. Woron*

ABOVE: Kathleen Gibson and skating buddies at James Baird State Park, 1960. *Courtesy David and Kathleen Ferris*

LEFT: The kindergarten class of St. Peter's School on Mill Street, Poughkeepsie, 1960. Sister John Maureen is on the left with Monsignor Francis Harper on the right. *Courtesy Peggy Ringwood*

OPPOSITE: Members of a veterans' group look on as Poughkeepsie Mayor Victor C. Waryas speaks during 1960 Veterans Day services at the Lincoln Center monument. *Courtesy Poughkeepsie Journal archives*

ABOVE: Family outing including the Lloyds, Cannings and Franks in Wappingers Falls, circa 1960. *Courtesy John M. Canning*

LEFT: Salt Point farmer Frank Susczynski (right) collects the first-place vegetable growing ribbon at the 1961 Dutchess County Fair from judge Walter "Andy" Androsko. Suscysnski owned Echo Hill Farm. *Courtesy Poughkeepsie Journal archives*

FAR LEFT: Main Street in Poughkeepsie is filled with cars and shoppers as the holidays approach in 1961. *Courtesy Poughkeepsie Journal archives*

OPPOSITE: Rombout Hunt Club members Bill Schermerhorn, Meg Kay, Richmond Meyer and Bill Carver, circa 1960. The photo was taken on Marshall Road in Pleasant Valley. *Courtesy Denise Byrnes*

RIGHT: Julie Lovelace, Fred Carpenter and Carol Dabros on Winnikee Avenue in April, 1961. *Courtesy Julie Lovelace Barilics*

FAR RIGHT: No doubt they'd rather be sledding or building snowmen but these children got a tougher assignment in January 1961 following a nine-inch snowfall in Poughkeepsie. Clockwise from left, are Frank Sculco III, Frances Sculco, John Sculco and Jerry Sculco. The car belonged to Frank's and Frances' father, Frank Sculco, Jr. John and Jerry are his nephews. *Courtesy Poughkeepsie Journal archives*

BELOW: There appears to be more apple on the boy than in the boy as Paul Wigsten, 6, of Pleasant Valley munches on a candied apple at the August 1961 Dutchess County Fair in Rhinebeck while visiting with Charles Traver, 9, of Poughkeepsie and his 4-H Guernsey calf, Betsy. *Courtesy Poughkeepsie Journal archives*

ABOVE: Well before gas prices even approached $1, Wappingers Falls resident Jack Barnard found an economic way to commute to his job at IBM in East Fishkill. Here, Barnard, a member of an international bicycle club, rides his vintage 10-speed down East Fishkill's Lake Walton Road in July 1961.
Courtesy Poughkeepsie Journal archives

LEFT: If you didn't have snowtires, it's likely you weren't going far in Poughkeepsie this day in February 1961.
Courtesy Poughkeepsie Journal archives

TOP LEFT: A 15-foot pile of discarded Christmas trees is set ablaze, sending flames 60 feet into the air in January 1961 at Poughkeepsie's Spratt Park. *Courtesy Poughkeepsie Journal archives*

ABOVE: Representing President Kennedy, General W.C. Westmoreland, who would later head U.S. forces in Vietnam, joins Eleanor Roosevelt and National Foundation poster child John MaGuire of Long Island to lay a wreath in January 1962 at the grave of late President Franklin D. Roosevelt in Hyde Park. At the time, Westmoreland was superintendent of the U.S. Military Academy at West Point. *Courtesy Poughkeepsie Journal archives*

TOP RIGHT: Bruce Dooris and Jimmy Sherman at the park on the corner of Riverview Field Street and Lincoln Avenue, 1962. This park is now called Stitzel Field Park. *Courtesy Dale Sherman*

MIDDLE RIGHT: In April 1962, the Spackenkill Parent-Teacher Association was honored to have Mrs. Eleanor Roosevelt as a guest speaker. To make the occasion even more special, the PTA Executive Board extended an invitation to their guest to an informal "covered dish" dinner, which she accepted. It was held in the cafeteria of the Croft Road School, which is now Orville Todd Junior High. The regular meeting followed in the gymnasium to a standing-room-only audience. Mrs. Roosevelt spoke to the crowd for well over an hour. *Courtesy Mildred D. Lay*

BOTTOM RIGHT: Cathy and Bobby Monell at the waterfront in Newburgh, 1962. *Courtesy Cathy Coppinger*

ABOVE: Fishkill Elementary School kindergarten class, 1962-63. The teacher was Ms. Persh and those known are John Borden (third from the left), John Feilen (sixth from the left), and Frank Licata (eighth from the left). *Courtesy June Feilen*

LEFT: Veterans Day 1963 generated plenty of talk about allies, foes and politics. Here, Congressman Hamilton Fish Sr. of Millbrook speaks at Lincoln Center ceremonies in Poughkeepsie about the struggle between communism and Christianity. *Courtesy Poughkeepsie Journal archives*

FAR LEFT: It's probably safe to say that Vincent Kane's artwork can't be matched. Here in September 1963, Kane shows off a schooner, submarine and cabin cruiser he constructed totally of matchsticks, while holding the framing for a larger cruiser he was building. *Courtesy Poughkeepsie Journal archives*

LEFT: The buildings look the same in November 1963 as they did years before, but here at the former Dutchess Bleachery in Wappingers Falls, much change has taken place. *Courtesy Poughkeepsie Journal archives*

BOTTOM LEFT: Home on leave in December 1963 are (left to right) airman apprentice Joseph Becchetti Jr. of Poughkeepsie, fireman Richard J. Semmelhack of Clintondale and seaman apprentice George W. Majestic of Gardiner. The three had just completed naval recruit training in Illinois. *Courtesy Poughkeepsie Journal archives*

BOTTOM MIDDLE: New Jersey Senator Clifford P. Case, a Poughkeepsie native, visits with his mother in April 1963 before speaking at the Arlington Senior High School Stockholders' Ball. *Courtesy Poughkeepsie Journal archives*

OPPOSITE: Kids help kids here in November 1961 as (front row, left to right) Joseph Sackelos, 5; Laura Sackelos, 2; and Gary Bradford, 3; and (back row, left to right) Terry Bradford, 5, and James Sackelos, 4, gather in the Sackelos' New Hamburg home with toys that would be given to the Salvation Army for distribution to needy children. *Courtesy Poughkeepsie Journal archives*

BELOW: Still fighting, but this time a different kind of battle, is Clove Valley resident Melvin Krulewitch. Krulewitch, a retired Marine general who fought in World War I, World War II and the Korean War, is pictured here in his home in June 1963, when he was battling corruption in boxing as chairman of the New York State Athletic Commission. *Courtesy Poughkeepsie Journal archives*

RIGHT: Reading for holidays, officers of the Our Lady of Lourdes High School Glee Club rehearse in late November of 1963. Left to right are co-president seniors Thomas Pasquazi and Barbara Joseph, freshman John Beltrane and, on piano, co-president Linda Dale Miles, a junior. *Courtesy Poughkeepsie Journal archives*

BOTTOM RIGHT: Hailed as heroes in May 1963 are (left to right) Poughkeepsie residents Joseph Farley, 8, Joseph Cioto, 11 and Louis Thomas, 10. With police barricading the city after a prisoner escaped custody outside the courthouse, the boys hailed a state police investigator to report they spotted the man near a restaurant under construction on Front Street. The man, who'd been convicted of grand larceny, was soon recaptured. *Courtesy Poughkeepsie Journal archives*

BOTTOM MIDDLE: Shad boning, a closely guarded art, is demonstrated here in May 1963 by longtime Hudson River fisherman Raymond Minard of Poughkeepsie. Minard didn't learn the technique until nearly 30 years after he first started fishing for shad. *Courtesy Poughkeepsie Journal archives*

BELOW: Noting that many blacks in Mississippi were being prevented from voting, Charles Evers (left), Mississippi field secretary of the NAACP, used a September 1963 dinner in Poughkeepsie honoring his slain brother, Medgar, to call for increased voter participation among Poughkeepsie's black population. He said the city's black residents had no excuse not to vote. Joining him here at the dinner, which was held at the IBM Country Club, is (center) Dr. William Abruzzi and (right) Rupert Tarver. Medgar Evars, a civil rights activist, was shot to death outside his Mississippi home earlier in 1963. *Courtesy Poughkeepsie Journal archives*

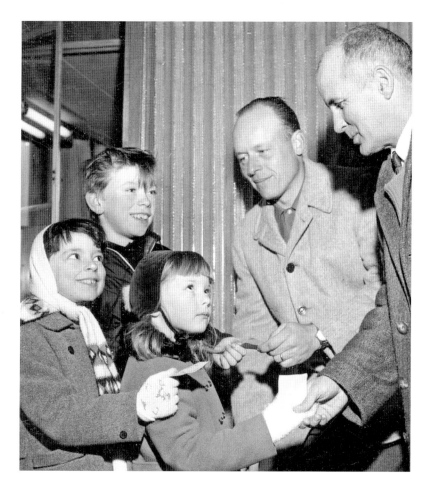

ABOVE: The nation mourned the death of President John F. Kennedy, following his assassination in November 1963. Here, Hyde Park resident Richard Marto pauses to view a black-draped portrait of the president at the Poughkeepsie Post Office. *Courtesy Poughkeepsie Journal archives*

TOP LEFT: Poughkeepsie Police Athletic League Vice President Fred Macky (second from right) and President Robert St. Germain (right) greet (from left) Karen Sculco, 8, her brother Jerry, 12, and sister, Donna, 6, at the PAL's annual children's Christmas party at the Bardavon Opera House in 1963. *Courtesy Poughkeepsie Journal archives*

LEFT: Pam and Gary Veeder wedding photo at Dutch Reformed Church in Poughkeepsie, July 28, 1963. *Courtesy Pam and Gary Veeder*

ABOVE: The Wappinger Creek floods "Brick Row," houses at Route 55 near Overlook Bridge, Poughkeepsie, 1963. *Courtesy David and Kathleen Ferris*

RIGHT: State police enforced a ban on games of chance but games of skill still provided plenty of fun at the July 1963 Millbrook Fire Department Carnival. Here, Karen Frenzel and Gerald Tellerday try ring toss as volunteer fireman James Hart looks on.

Courtesy Poughkeepsie Journal archives

ABOVE: These young Poughkeepsie fishermen proved to be the "reel" deal, hauling six rainbow trout out of the Ashokan Reservoir near Kingston in April 1965. Left is Bob Kochis and right is his brother, Ronald. *Courtesy Poughkeepsie Journal archives*

ABOVE LEFT: Holstein calves stand for judging at the August 1963 Dutchess County Fair. *Courtesy Poughkeepsie Journal archives*

LEFT: The civil rights movement still had a long way to go in December 1964 when Dick Gregory (left), a leading voice for equality, appeared at Vassar College. Here, he poses with students Judy Allen (center) of California and Gay Nicholl (right) of Connecticut, members of the Student Activities Committee, which sponsored his appearance. *Courtesy Poughkeepsie Journal archives*

RIGHT: Louis Nicolik of Poughkeepsie might have been fishing for shad but he opted not to throw back this 35-pound striped bass that made its way into his net in the Hudson River in May 1964. Nicolik, who was fishing with his brother, Leo, said the 40-inch fish was the largest he'd ever caught.
Courtesy Poughkeepsie Journal archives

FAR RIGHT: They may all look alike, but Michael Drugan has no problem finding his mailbox among the 60 located together on Route 52 in Fishkill in October 1964.
Courtesy Poughkeepsie Journal archives

BELOW: Cleaning up fall leaves is a big job. And here, in 1964, one big homemade contraption is used by Town of Poughkeepsie resident David Wengen to handle the task. Wengen's father, Henry, vice president of engineering and research at Fargo Manufacturing Company, built the machine, explaining he simply got tired of raking. *Courtesy Poughkeepsie Journal archives*

LEFT: Santa (or at least Santa's local helper, Alfred Ironside of the Town of Poughkeepsie) gives toys to Clintondale 4-year-olds Roseann Hayes (center) and Rosemarie Dunn (right) as Mrs. Donald Perkins looks on. The AFL-CIO United Auto Workers hosted the Christmas party at Poughkeepsie High School for the children. *Courtesy Poughkeepsie Journal archives*

FAR LEFT: Keeping their peers safe in January 1964 is the job of these Rombout School students in Beacon. The boys, (seated, left to right) Lawrence Dowd and Kenneth Siebert and standing, (left to right) Frank Riess and Dale Mosher, are members of the Patrol Boys organization, which directs traffic.
Courtesy Poughkeepsie Journal archives

BELOW: Vassar Brothers Hospital's laboratory went under the microscope in February 1964 and gained American Society of Clinical Pathologists' approval as a school for certified laboratory assistants. Here in the lab are (seated) Helen Tsitsera, hematology; and standing, left to right, Jessmine Roberts, bio-chemistry; Janet Arnold, senior instructor; Dorothea Underhill, histology; and Lillian Babcock, senior bacteriologist. *Courtesy Poughkeepsie Journal archives*

RIGHT: $170,198 was the then-sizeable amount of money paid in 1964 for 11 new Dutchess County Highway Department trucks. The fleet additions are parked in August of that year behind (left to right) Highway Superintendent Edgar M. Petrovits and Board of Supervisors members Rocco T. DiGilio of Poughkeepsie and Cecil Sherow of Pleasant Valley. *Courtesy Poughkeepsie Journal archives*

BOTTOM RIGHT: Judge Walter Androsko (left) tries to decide which is the most perfect pumpkin and which is the most terrific tomato during the 1964 Dutchess County Fair as vegetable exhibit superintendent Frank Susczynski and his daughter, Irene, 13, look on. *Courtesy Poughkeepsie Journal archives*

OPPOSITE: Giving new definition to the term farmhand, (left to right) Richard Varney of Pleasant Valley, William Hewlett of Poughkeepsie, Charles Traver of Poughkeepsie and William's brother, Richard, keep themselves occupied as rain falls at the 1964 Dutchess County Fair. *Courtesy Poughkeepsie Journal archives*

BELOW: Poughkeepsie Day School Music Director Dinwall Fleary (left) plays the harpsichord as Roberta Levine, a Vassar College music major, plays the flute during a concert at Poughkeepsie Day School in October 1964. The harpsichord was build by Dr. and Mrs. Dwight W. Chapman, Jr. of Vassar. *Courtesy Poughkeepsie Journal archives*

RIGHT: Going the way of history in January 1964 is St. Joseph's School, a Poughkeepsie landmark. The school, located on Mansion Street, was founded in 1916 for the children of Polish descent by four sisters of the Congregation of the Resurrection. In 1960, the school was merged with Nativity Parish School on Union Street. *Courtesy Poughkeepsie Journal archives*

BELOW: Flying was no mere flight of fancy in November 1964 for 16-year-old Red Hook youths Michael Fisher (left) and Michael Lockhart (right). The two Red Hook Central School students both soloed in Rhinebeck and, at the time, were working toward their private pilot's licenses. *Courtesy Poughkeepsie Journal archives*

RIGHT: Lady Bird Johnson, wife of President Lyndon B. Johnson, visits the Roosevelt Library in Hyde Park with Amenia resident Mary Lasker in July 1965. Johnson, a flower lover, spent more than four decades advocating beautification projects throughout the country. In 1965, Lasker donated 9,000 bushes and plants to beautify Washington, D.C.'s Pennsylvania Avenue.
Courtesy Poughkeepsie Journal archives

FAR RIGHT: Sunshine falls on the graves of President Franklin D. Roosevelt and his wife, Eleanor, in Hyde Park in 1965. April 12, 1965 marked the 20th anniversary of FDR's death.
Courtesy Poughkeepsie Journal archives

BELOW: Laying the foundation for future victories, workers at Dutchess Community College in the Town of Poughkeepsie work on the site of the school's new gym in May 1965. To that point, the college's home contests were played off-campus, including at Spackenkill High School. *Courtesy Poughkeepsie Journal archives*

LEFT: Pitching the 1965 New York World's Fair is former Yankee ace Allie Reynolds. Here, Reynolds, who was working at one of the fair's pavilions, shows Robert DiDomizio, 10, of Wappingers Falls, one of his grips. *Courtesy Poughkeepsie Journal archives*

FAR LEFT: It's called a snorkel but it has nothing to do with underwater exploration. Instead, this 70-foot-long apparatus is used for firefighting and rescue. Local officials, including Mayor Victor C. Waryas, get a ride skyward during a demonstration at Dutton Lumber Company in Poughkeepsie.
Courtesy Poughkeepsie Journal archives

ABOVE LEFT: It's lights, camera and, thankfully, full power in November 1965, as Harry Briggs, operator/caretaker of the Niagara Mohawk power station in Pleasant Valley, checks the switching station after power was restored following a massive blackout.
Courtesy Poughkeepsie Journal archives

ABOVE RIGHT: The Dodgers might have been long gone from Brooklyn but in July 1965, New York still had a team of lovable losers in the Mets. The glory days were still four years away here when Hopewell resident Michael A. Cannizzaro (right) visited with "The Old Professor," Manager Casey Stengel, at Shea Stadium. Cannizzaro was due to co-sponsor an upcoming Mets' tryout camp in Peekskill.
Courtesy Poughkeepsie Journal archives

ABOVE: IBM facility near Building 002, Route 9, 1948.
Courtesy Timothy P. Holls

RIGHT: Newly elected Union Vale Supervisor Donald Wisseman helps ready his house for Christmas in December 1965 with family members. Wisseman, a former Pittsburgh Pirate farmhand who owned a 340-acre Union Vale/LaGrangeville dairy farm with his two brothers, is joined by his wife (seated) and children, left to right, Barry, Mary Lou and Donald Jr.
Courtesy Poughkeepsie Journal archives

BELOW: Signaling the area's growth surge, traffic lights appear for the first time at the intersection of Raymond and College avenues in Poughkeepsie. The lights were installed after the intersection was widened to four lanes. In the background is the Vassar College Alumnae House. *Courtesy Poughkeepsie Journal archives*

ABOVE: A freight train rumbles over the new arterial highway that connects Poughkeepsie's Hoffman Street (far left) with North Water Street (far right) in July 1965. *Courtesy Poughkeepsie Journal archives*

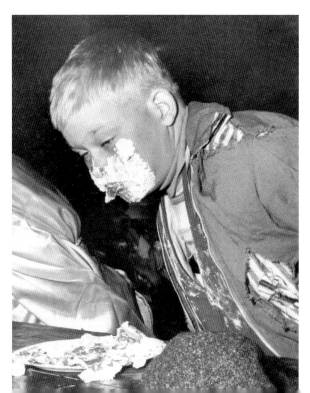

ABOVE: Mrs. Frederick P. Wilcox (right), who donated her 660-acre Milan farm to Dutchess County as parkland to honor her late husband, speaks with Amenia resident James Place (left) in July 1965 during the annual Town-Country Days farm tour. Place's father worked on the farm and Place grew up on it. Behind them is Red Hook farmer Robert G. Greig, the day's master of ceremonies, who was vice president of the State Farm Bureau. *Courtesy Poughkeepsie Journal archives*

LEFT: Halloween generally means lots of candy, but here William Miller, 12, of Poughkeepsie celebrates the holiday with pie during the city's 15th annual Halloween party. Miller ate half a pie in little more than a minute to take top pie-eating honors. *Courtesy Poughkeepsie Journal archives*

FAR LEFT: It wasn't really good enough to eat but this model of the Joseph T. Tower Nurses Residence at Vassar Hospital in Poughkeepsie was good enough to win a special recognition award in 1965 in the hospital's annual Christmas decoration contest. Here, Judith Boldvay, the hospital's director of residences, applies finishing touches to the project, which was constructed out of wax paper, crepe paper and sugar frosting. *Courtesy Poughkeepsie Journal archives*

RIGHT: Fired up about their school, Bennett College freshmen Patty Clay (left) and Tanny Madira (right) ride in the college's 75th anniversary parade along Route 44 in Millbrook in May 1966. *Courtesy Poughkeepsie Journal archives*

BOTTOM RIGHT: A slider, a change or even a spitter, it's hard to tell here as Mayor Richard Mitchell prepares to throw out the opening pitch at Eastman Oval to mark the start of the 1966 Poughkeepsie Little League Association season. *Courtesy Poughkeepsie Journal archives*

BELOW: After chalking up a win, famed billiards expert Steve Mizerak (right) looks on as three-time World Pocket Billiards Champion Irving Crane (left) lines up a shot at the Game Room in Poughkeepsie in September 1965. Mizerak, 20, defeated Crane 200-146 in an exhibition. *Courtesy Poughkeepsie Journal archives*

LEFT: Before opening ceremonies, Hudson River Valley Commission Chairman Frank Wells McCabe (left) and City Manager Theodore Maurer (right) look over a road to the future, the new north-south arterial highway in Poughkeepsie at South Avenue and Academy Street, in September 1966.
Courtesy Poughkeepsie Journal archives

BOTTOM LEFT: There was a time when iceboating dominated the winter sports scene in the Hudson Valley. Here in 1966, Roosevelt Library police officer Charles Kane looks at part of the Icicle, once a 69-foot-long craft built in Poughkeepsie for Franklin Roosevelt's uncle, John Roosevelt, from wood on the Roosevelt Hyde Park estate. The boat, which was clocked at more than 100 mph, won national titles on the Hudson four times in the late 1800s. *Courtesy Poughkeepsie Journal archives*

BELOW: Car maven Alice Huyler Ramsey, a former Vassar College student, and California resident, made history in 1909 by becoming the first woman to drive across the United States. Ramsey, pictured here at the Vassar Alumnae House in July 1966, stopped in Poughkeepsie with her two passengers, her sisters-in-law, during that historic drive from Manhattan to San Francisco. Driving a four-cylinder Maxwell, her 60-day trip (41 actually spent on the road) received wide news coverage. The group had to change 11 tires while crossing unpaved desert and more. Ramsey made more than 20 subsequent cross-country drives, one in 1969, when she noted she hit 75 mph in her Mercedes en route from California to her 62nd class reunion at Vassar. *Courtesy Poughkeepsie Journal archives*

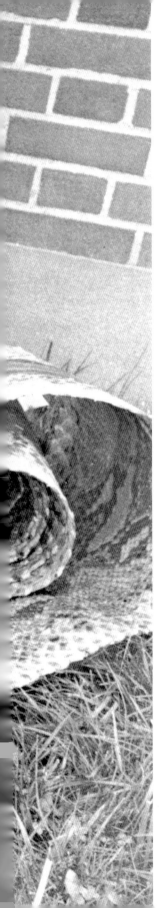

LEFT: On their way to Albany in June 1966 are (sitting, left to right) Linda Maile of Pawling, Francena Osoba of Beacon and Lilli Weigert of Poughkeepsie and (standing, left to right) Toni Grote of Tivoli, Kimberly Culver of Amenia and Joanne Sartori of Dover Plains. The American Legion Ladies Auxiliary chose the girls to attend the 51st annual Girls' State program. *Courtesy Poughkeepsie Journal archives*

BOTTOM LEFT: Number 1,000 at Vassar Hospital but number one in his mother's heart is five-day-old James Louis Staffa Jr., shown here at home with his mother, Linda Staffa, on July 22, 1966. The baby was the 1,000th born that year at the Poughkeepsie hospital. A picture of his Marine father sits behind him. Private First Class Staffa was en route to Vietnam at the time this photo was taken.
Courtesy Poughkeepsie Journal archives

OPPOSITE: It's meet the reptiles—or at least their skins—day for kindergarteners at Pleasant Valley Elementary School in November 1967. Pictured from left, Kippy Stewart, Wendell Folwer, Cathy Bishop and Louise Mima examine a sea turtle shell, the skin of a West Indies lizard and the skin of a 22-foot boa constrictor. *Courtesy Poughkeepsie Journal archives*

BELOW: Francis Cardinal Spellman blesses students at St. Columba School in Hopewell Junction in September 1966. The archbishop was on hand to dedicate the school's new building.
Courtesy Poughkeepsie Journal archives

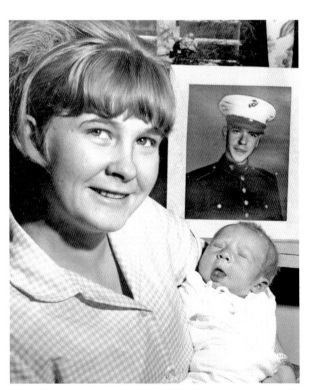

ABOVE: Few embraced the age of Aquarius more than Dr. Timothy Leary. Here, the barefoot doctor and his wife, Rosemary Woodruff, smile after exchanging vows in a Hindu/western ceremony in Millbrook in December 1967. The ceremony was the second for the couple, who were first married in the California desert. *Courtesy Poughkeepsie Journal archives*

TOP RIGHT: Mayor Charles Wolf and members of the Beacon City Council at the dedication of the Beacon Car Wash, 1966. From left, Joseph Stella, Mayor Charles Wolf, Taylor Edwards, car wash owner Luigi DeDominicis and Tom Forman. De Dominicis was an Italian immigrant who became one of the most successful business owners in Beacon. *Courtesy Peter Forman*

RIGHT: God's house is in the big house here as prisoners, area clergy and state and local officials attend the dedication Mass October 13, 1967 of the new chapel inmates and prison officers constructed at Green Haven prison. The building was dedicated as St. Paul's Chapel. *Courtesy Poughkeepsie Journal archives*

ABOVE: With an eye toward safety, Beacon Police Lieutenant George Garrison shows Jan Beaudway, 13, of Wappinger, how to inspect his gun barrel during an October 1967 course at the Dutchess and Putnam Sportsmen's Association in Fishkill.
Courtesy Poughkeepsie Journal archives

LEFT: It's out with the old as buildings are demolished at the foot of Union Street and Union Square in Poughkeepsie in May 1967. The work was part of a large, 74-acre urban renewal project.
Courtesy Poughkeepsie Journal archives

TOP LEFT: Music director Calude Monteux, soloist Eugene Istomin (center) and the rest of the 75-piece Hudson Valley Philharmonic Orchestra stand to receive applause after kicking off the orchestra's ninth season with a performance in October 1967. *Courtesy Poughkeepsie Journal archives*

RIGHT: "Rocky," New York Governor Nelson A. Rockefeller (second from left), who'd later become vice president of the United States, visits the offices of the Poughkeepsie Journal in September 1967. To his right is Publisher Edward J. Quilla. To his left are Arthur F. Wollenhaupt, newspaper president; Edwin H. Rozell, editorial director; and State Senator Jay P. Rolison (hand extended). *Courtesy Poughkeepsie Journal archives*

BELOW: Work on the new, $239,000 LaGrange Town Hall is well under way here in November 1967. *Courtesy Poughkeepsie Journal archives*

ABOVE: What handicap? That might be the question asked about 15-year-old Roger Bastian of Poughkeepsie. Born with a partially developed left arm, Bastian, shown taking aim here in July 1968, won the 1967 Dutchess Bowmen's youth championship.
Courtesy Poughkeepsie Journal archives

ABOVE LEFT: Baring teeth but only in a friendly manner, members of the Dutchess County Sheriff's Office's canine corps look ready for action in July 1967. Left to right are Thunder, with Sergeant George Rymph; Butch, with Acting Sergeant Henry Small; and King, with Sheriff Lawrence M. Quinlan. *Courtesy Poughkeepsie Journal archives*

LEFT: Poughkeepsie's winning swimmers display their trophies in August 1968 following the city swim meet. Front row, left to right, are Carol Kennedy, Darcy Anderson, Marueen Ryan, Mike McCombs and Kevin Connell. Back row, left to right, are Jack Kennedy, Robert Brooke, Barbara Kennedy, Betsy Kennedy and Stephen Knauss.
Courtesy Poughkeepsie Journal archives

ABOVE: Toasting the occasion with a shared soda, Carl Chapin, 6, of Ancram (right) and his buddy, Sheila MacArthur, 5, (left) of Ancram watch a parade celebrating the Town of Stanford's 175th anniversary in September 1968. *Courtesy Poughkeepsie Journal archives*

ABOVE LEFT: "Dr. J," Julius Erving, would ultimately be recognized as the league's big name but in 1968, Poughkeepsie native Wes Bialosuknia was drawing headlines with the American Basketball Association's Oakland Oaks. Bialosuknia (right) shows Poughkeepsie Journal Sports Editor John Flanagan the Jaguar he received as part of his 1967 Oaks' contract. The big man, who starred for the University of Connecticut Huskies, was great from the outside, setting an ABA record by sinking nine consecutive three-pointers. *Courtesy Poughkeepsie Journal archives*

LEFT: Detroit Tiger pitcher Fred Lasher (center) receives the key to Poughkeepsie from Mayor Richard W. Mitchell (left) in February 1969. Lasher, a former Poughkeepsie High and Poughkeepsie Twilight League player, was slated to help at an upcoming YMCA baseball clinic. At right is Donald J. McKiernan, YMCA associate general secretary. *Courtesy Poughkeepsie Journal archives*

ABOVE: Shad fisherman Alfred E. Storms, 41, of Marlboro prepares a net with the help of William W. Tubbs, 18, (background) of Marlboro near the Hudson River in Poughkeepsie in May 1967. *Courtesy Poughkeepsie Journal archives*

LEFT: Showing strength and form, members of the new Poughkeepsie Civic Ballet Company practice in November 1967. Left to right are Jackie Solotar, 18, of Fishkill; Michele Ribble, 14, of Poughkeepsie; Denise Costine, 15, of LaGrangeville; and Kathy Jackson, 15, of LaGrangeville. *Courtesy Poughkeepsie Journal archives*

FAR LEFT: Members of the Neighborhood Youth Corps climb the 90-foot Stissing Mountain fire tower in Pine Plains in July 1967. Foreman Roy Sagarin of Pine Plains oversaw the teenagers' work at the site. *Courtesy Poughkeepsie Journal archives*

TOP: Pine Plains resident Roy Sagarin, the foreman at the Stissing Mountain fire tower in Pine Plains, stands with his summer work crew in July 1967. The boys, (standing, left to right) Al Boone and Pancho Greklek and (seated, left to right) John Melious and Jerry Sculco, got the assignment through the Neighborhood Youth Corps *Courtesy Poughkeepsie Journal archives*

ABOVE: The formal opening of the new Market Street home of Merrill Lynch, Pierce, Fenner and Smith in Poughkeepsie was slated for March 14, 1968 but Rudy Vincenti is already at his desk working a day earlier. *Courtesy Poughkeepsie Journal archives*

RIGHT: Preserving recreation space was even a concern 40 years ago. Here, state Senator Jay P. Rolison, Jr. (left), a member of the Joint Legislative Committee on Conservation of Natural Resources, joins 60 other riders, including (right) Mrs. Frederick Hicks and (behind) Mrs. George Verilli, at the dedication of the Landsman Kill Trail Association's new horse trails in Rhinebeck. *Courtesy Poughkeepsie Journal archives*

ABOVE: Well, hello...Barbra... Two of Hollywood's all-time biggest names, Barbra Streisand and Gene Kelly, discuss a scene while filming Hello Dolly at the Poughkeepsie Railroad Station in July 1968. Kelly directed the picture, which was also shot in Yonkers and Garrison. *Courtesy Poughkeepsie Journal archives*

LEFT: Dressed in period costumes, actors mill around the Poughkeepsie Railroad Station platform near a coal-burning train during the shooting of a scene for the movie Hello Dolly in July 1968. The overhead screening was designed to soften bright sunlight. *Courtesy Poughkeepsie Journal archives*

ABOVE: Lorri Creighton, 14, Mary Howard, 14, and Laurie Singer, 15, play with children at the First Baptist Church daycare center in Poughkeepsie in the summer of 1968. The girls volunteered at the center through a county-run program.
Courtesy Poughkeepsie Journal archives

OPPOSITE: In a not-your-everyday scene, an amphibious car is driven toward the replica of a racing schooner that's visiting Poughkeepsie in September 1968. The car was owned by Francis Peters of Poughkeepsie and the schooner by F&M Schaefer Brewing Company. The seaplane (right) belonged to two college students, who landed to see what was going on.
Courtesy Poughkeepsie Journal archives

LEFT: Wappingers Falls may be just a small dot on the map in the scheme of things nationally but in May 1969, Theodore C. Sorensen (right), White House aide to President John F. Kennedy, attended the town Democratic Party's victory dinner, held at the Knights of Columbus Hall. Mayor Peter C. Furnari is pictured here with Sorensen. *Courtesy Poughkeepsie Journal archives*

ABOVE: Sherry Daniels (second from right) claims her sixth Poughkeepsie Area Tennis Tournament championship trophy in eight years after recapturing the women's singles title in July 1968 by defeating Carol Gordon (second from left), 6-3, 6-4, at Poughkeepsie High School. Left is tournament chairman John R. Heilman, Jr. At right is Mrs. Marie Tarver, vice president of the Poughkeepsie Board of Education. *Courtesy Poughkeepsie Journal archives*

BELOW: Arlington firemen lead the 22nd annual Dutchess County Volunteer Firemen's Parade in Arlington in July 1968. *Courtesy Poughkeepsie Journal archives*

ABOVE: A band plays at Frivolous Sal's Saloon in Poughkeepsie, 1968. In front, from left, co-owners, Mike Chiriatti and Larry Plover, and in back are Roger Fay and Jim Leary. *Courtesy Larry Plover*

BELOW: Six-year-old Henry Fox Jr. holds the American flag as he watches fire engines pass during the 22nd annual Dutchess County Volunteer Firemen's Parade in Arlington in July 1968. *Courtesy Poughkeepsie Journal archives*

LEFT: A mailman's best friends? Breaking stereotype, Blackie and Peggy aren't sizing up Poughkeepsie postman John McKenna as a potential breakfast snack, but are merely following him on his route in September 1968—something they'd done at this point every day for three years. The caring canines hooked up with McKenna at the same location, no matter the weather. McKenna inherited the duo from the previous letter carrier, who was granted the same escort. *Courtesy Poughkeepsie Journal archives*

FAR LEFT: Display window of Di Pleco Tailors in Mount Carmel Square, Poughkeepsie, circa 1968. *Courtesy Randy Ross*

BOTTOM LEFT: Part of a burned plane that crashed in Mesier Park in Wappingers Falls in February 1968 lies next to a damaged car. *Courtesy Poughkeepsie Journal archives*

BELOW: Area residents look at a small plane that slammed into a tree in Mesier Park in Wappingers Falls in February 1968, killing three people. *Courtesy Poughkeepsie Journal archives*

TOP: Oscar "Ike" Boone, with hat, accepts the Genesee Trophy for winning Sunday's day of golf at the College Hill course. Others are, from left, professional Jack Gleason; second-place winner Frank Abbott; Joe Natoli, Genesee Brewing Company representative; and Ed Edelman of Bridge City Beer Distributors, local Genesee distributors, May 1960.
Courtesy Jack Gleason

ABOVE: Some heavy hitters tour the Western Publishing and Lithographing Company in January 1968. Here, plant manager William Howe shows a book to heavyweight boxer Jim Howard (left), trainer Joe Fariello, heavyweight Buster Mathis and the world's third-ranked middleweight, Benny Briscoe. Mathis, who trained with Howard in Hyde Park, had the distinction of losing to two of the biggest names in the sport, Joe Frazier and Muhammad Ali.
Courtesy Poughkeepsie Journal archives

RIGHT: For most of his life, Dana Blafield (center) of Pleasant Valley battled a heart condition. But in 1967, the 16-year-old was cleared to play baseball and also was chosen to be an honorary Yankee batboy one July day. Here, Blafield poses at Yankee Stadium with his hero, Mickey Mantle, and another unidentified youngster.
Courtesy Poughkeepsie Journal archives

ABOVE: Three times the fun was had in July 1969, as (left to right) triplets Timothy, Ann Marie and Bernadette McGinnis celebrate their 10th birthdays at their Town of Pougkeepsie home.
Courtesy Poughkeepsie Journal archives

ABOVE: Santa arrives early and is warmly received as he hands out gifts to 250 children December 13, 1969, at the Bardavon theater in Poughkeepsie. The event was sponsored by the Salvation Army. *Courtesy Poughkeepsie Journal archives*

RIGHT: Mirroring protests throughout the country, an estimated 5,000 marchers descend on downtown Poughkeepsie in October 1969 to call for the withdrawal of U.S. forces from Vietnam. The march was part of Vietnam Moratorium Day. *Courtesy Poughkeepsie Journal archives*

BELOW: Diana, Scott and Judy digging snow tunnels in front of 47 Scenic Drive in Poughkeepsie on February 19, 1969. *Courtesy Richard and Anna Suko*

ABOVE: The need for accessibility for the disabled was just starting to be recognized in the 1960s. Here in July 1969, members of Vassar Construction Corporation build a ramp to the Poughkeepsie Post Office. *Courtesy Poughkeepsie Journal archives*

LEFT: American pride is evident on Hoffman Avenue in Poughkeepsie as residents celebrate the July 1969 moon landing by flying the American flag outside their homes. Here (left to right), Hoffman Avenue children Lois Lezon, 7, Sharon Seifts, 10, Timothy Masten, 8, and Sharon's brother, David, 9, admire the display, while Lois also cuddles a kitty. *Courtesy Poughkeepsie Journal archives*

TOP LEFT: It's impossible to see in a black and white photo but Easter, the chicken, was one special bird -- or, at least, her eggs were special. Easter, pictured here with her owner, Ernest H. Adams of Beekman in March 1969, confounded Adams and others by laying blue-shelled eggs. *Courtesy Poughkeepsie Journal archives*

TOP MIDDLE: First Baptist Church choir in the fall of 1969. Third from left in the front row is choir director Al Hunter. *Courtesy Richard and Anna Suko*

Index

1940s introduction, 7
1950s introduction, 59
1960s introduction, 95

Abbott, Frank, 138
Abruzzi, William, 108
Acker, Terry, 73
Ackerman, Dorothy, 49
Ackerman, Dot, 73
Adams, Ernest H., 141
Adams, Robin, 38
Adler, Charles H., 69
airplane crash (Wappingers Falls), 137
Aldrich, Raymond E., Jr., 26
Alexander Hamilton (vessel), 66
Aliotta, Jacke, 35
Aliotta, Joanne, 35
Allen, Bill, 25
Allen, Judy, 111
Amenia High School, 8
Amenia Town Hall and Fire Department building, 21
American Cancer Society fundraising, 74
American Grand National dog race, 77
American Legion Lafayette Post, 46
American Red Cross dinner, 69
amphibious car, 134–35
Anderson, Alec "Sandy," 44
Anderson, Caroline, 48
Anderson, Darcy, 129
Anderson, Lubin, 20
Andrews, Agnes, 54
Andrews, Jeff, 54
Andrews, Jim, 54
Andrews, Mae, 54
Andrews, Tom, 54
Androsko, Walter "Andy," 101, 114
apartment building fire, 70
Arlington High football team, 34
Arlington Speedway, 97
Armistice Day celebration, 14–15
Armstrong, Dolores, 67
Armstrong, Earl, 67
Armstrong, Truman "Bab," 44
Arnold, Janet, 113
Autry, Gene, 63
Avello, John, 62
Awosting Falls, 91

Babcock, Lillian, 113
Babiarz, John, 62
Baer, Emil, 17
Balassone, George, 16
Bardavon Theater, 140
Barden, Jimmy, 23
Barnard, Jack, 103
Barr, Terry, 44
Barrytown Railroad Station, 79
Bartel, Pauline, 86–87
Bastian, Roger, 129
Beacon, Mr., 16
Beacon City Council, 126

Beacon High School, 95
Beacon Laundry, 17
Beatty, David, 43
Beaudway, Jan, 127
Becchetti, Joseph, Jr., 107
Becchetti, Rosemarie, 43
Beckett, Barbara Hammond, 24
bed and breakfast, 75
Beltrane, John, 108
Benack, Alfred, 27
Benario, Herbert, 50
Bennett, Austin "Audie," 21
Bennett, Monroe, 21
Bennett, Preston, 21
Bennett College anniversary parade, 122
Bentley, Austin, 91
Bergman, Deborah, 24
Bernzweig, Myra, 24
Berthelot, John, 50
Best, Edna, 17
Bettina, Melio, 8
Betz, Tillie, 73
Bialosuknia, Wes, 130
Billows, Ray, 51
Bilyou, Sheila, 78
Bishop, Cathy, 124–25
Blafield, Dana, 138
Blanchard, Caroline, 48
Blanchard, James, 48
Blanchard, Patricia, 48
Blanchard, Robert, 48
Blazejewski, Sally, 73
Blodgett Farm (Fishkill), 56
Bloom, Barbara, 24
Bloomer, Stan, 25
Blue Jays Football Team, 55
Bocchino, John, 64
Bogart, Joseph, Jr., 51
Bohlinger, Albert, 67
Bohlinger, Ellsworth, Jr., 67
Bohlinger, Ellsworth, Sr., 67
Bohlinger, Ellsworth Bay, Jr., 30
Bohlinger, George, 67
Bohlinger, Harold, 67
Boice, Lee, 33
Boice, Mae, 33
Boice, Pam, 35
Boldvay, Judith, 121
Bolin, Lionel, 23
bonfires, 61, 103
Boone, Al, 132
Boone, Oscar, 30
Boone, Oscar "Ike," 138
Borden, John, 105
Borst, Kermit, 16
Bowe, Maura, 41
Boy Scouts, 16, 28
Bradford, Gary, 106
Bradford, Sonny, 21
Bradford, Terry, 106
Briggs, Harry, 119

Briscoe, Benny, 138
Brooke, Robert, 129
Brophy, Jack, 25
Brophy, John, 16
Brower, Earl, 10
Brown, Bill, 8
Brown, Elmer Gunce, 27
Buck, Clifford M., 94–95
Burks, Louisa, 84
Burr, Mrs. Robert, 44
Byrd, Rev. Charles E., 54
Byrnes Message Bureau switchboard, 89

Cady, Bob "Two Gun," 25
Callahan, William, 35
Callender, Mrs. Robert, 23
Campbell, Barbara, 79
Campbell, Carole, 79
Campbell, Ingeborg, 79
Campbell, Marjorie, 79
Campbell, Richard, Jr., 79
Campbell, Richard, Sr., 79
Campitelli, Dorothy, 10
Cannings family, 101
Cannizzaro, Michael A., 119
Capano, Rose, 26
Capen, Gregory, 86–87
Cardinal Farley Military Academy (Rhinecliff), 83
Carlon, James, 43
Carnera, Primo, 47
Carpenter, Fred, 102
Carter, Mrs. E. Sterling, 44
Caruso, Concetta, 62
Caruso farm, 62
Carver, Bill, 100
Cary, Donald, 61
Case, Clifford P., 107
Casement, Mike, 35
Catharine Street Community Center, 24, 54
Cecchini, Al "Chick," 44
Cecchini, Mrs. Alfred, Sr., 44
Chamuras, Billy, 23
Chapin, Carl, 130
Charter, Carl "Jake," 62
Chartier, Grace, 72
cherry pie contest winner, 79
Chick, Marilyn, 73
Children's Home (Fairview), 44
Chiriatti, Mike, 136
Chocianowsky, Mr., 96
Christmas events, 13, 44, 89, 109, 113, 140
Chuck, Ellen, 49
Ciancanelli, Urbino "Worby," 17
Cioto, Joseph, 108
civil rights movement, 59, 108, 111
Clark, Bill, 50
Clark, P.J., 77
Clark, William, 75

Clay, Patty, 122
Clinton Corners, 12
Clinton Square, 47
Close, C. Fred, 38
Coast Guard cutter, 92–93
Cody, Father Peter, 88
Cohen, Betty, 24
Cohen, Grace, 24
Cohen, Judy, 24
Columbia Scholastic Press Association Superior Award, 49
Community War Chest, 28
Compasso, Martin, 81
Conklin, Ralph, 68
Conn, Billy, 8
Connell, Kevin, 129
coon dogs, 77
Corcoran, James, 10
Corey, Delores, 59–60
Cornelius, Chick, 21, 30
Costine, Denise, 131
Coughlin, Bob, 27, 32
Craig, Ruth, 75
Crane, Irving, 122
Creighton, Lorri, 135
Crodelle, Raymond, 43
Crooks, Dennis, 16
Crooks, Donald, 16
Crowell, Cliff, 77
Crowley, Joseph, 55
Crowley, Kenneth Dean, 55
Culver, Kimberly, 125

Dabros, Carol, 102
D'Angelo, Tony, 34
D'Angelo, Vincent, 34
Daniels, Sherry, 136
Davis, Victor, 43
Davisa, George, Jr., 16
Day, Helen, 84
Dean, Mrs. Harold R., 54
DeDominicis, Luigi, 126
DeFidi, Horatio, 35
DeFidi, Sylvia, 35
Dehart, Honin L., 9
Delamater, Malcolm, 51
Delsanto, Louis "Butch," 33
Democratic women's clubs, 11
Denning, Arthy, 55
Derby Playground Junior and Midget League Championships, 64–65
Deuell, F. Paul, 69
Devan, Toby, 49
Devorscik, John, 10
Dewey, Mrs. Thomas E., 52
Dewey, Thomas E., 52, 55
DiDomizio, Robert, 119
Diesing Supply Co., 54, 77
Dietrick, Margaret, 43
DiGilio, Rocco T., 114
Dinerstein, Marion, 24

DiPleco Tailors, 137
Di Santis, Bobbie, 15
Doelling, William, 61
dogs escorting mailman, 137
Dolan, Bobbie, 15
Domin, Jo Ann, 84
Domin, Joseph C., 32
Domin, Kathy, 84
Dongan Square, 67
Dooris, Bruce, 104
Dorchester Arms Motel, 49
Doughty, William, 23
Dow, James, 16
Dowd, Lawrence, 113
Dowdell, Florence, 50
Downey, Anna, 8
Dragstra, William, 16
Drake, Albert, 28
Drake, Richard, 15
Drugan, Michael, 112
Dubois, Edmund, 28
Duffy, Joe, 20
Duncan, Ernie, Jr., 21, 30
Duncan, Ernie, Sr., 21, 30
Dunn, Rosemarie, 113
Dutchess and Putnam Sportsmen's Association (Fishkill), 127
Dutchess Bleachery (Wappingers Falls), 107
Dutchess Community College, 118
Dutchess County Airport, 10, 66
Dutchess County American Red Cross dinner, 69
Dutchess County Fair, 101, 102, 111, 115
Dutchess County Health Association, 78
Dutchess County Highway Department, 114
Dutchess County Pistol Association, 29
Dutchess County Sheriff's Office canine corp, 129
Dutchess County Volunteer Firemen's Parade (Arlington), 136
Dutchess Divers, 81
Dutchess Fair, 45
Dutton Lumber Co., 119

Easter, the chicken, 141
Ebeling, Helen, 16
Edelman, Ed, 138
Edgar, Jane, 70
educational television, 86–87
Edwards, John L., 96
Edwards, Konrad, 86–87
Edwards, Taylor, 126
Effron, James, 43
Eisenhower, Dwight D., 59
Eisert, Rudy, 29
Eitzen, Jay, 59–60
Elton, Joseph, 34
Emery, Henry, 84

Emery & Webb, Inc., 84
Evening Star delivery boys, 13
Evers, Charles, 108

Fariello, Joe, 138
Farley, Harold, 72
Farley, Joseph, 108
Fay, Gerald, 23
Fay, Roger, 136
Feilen, John, 105
Ferris, Davis, 74
Ferris, Robert, 74
Fichtell, Bill, 44
Filoia, Sarah, 41
Finn, Buddy, 20
fires, 70
First Baptist Church, 83, 135, 141
Fish, Hamilton, Sr., 105
Fish, Karlene, 61
Fish, Louis, Jr., 61
Fish Creek wood bridge, 75
Fisher, Michael, 116
fishing, 111, 112, 131
Fishkill Elementary School, 105
Fishman, Lonnie, 91
Fitchett, Carlton B., 16
Flanagan, John, 130
Flannery, J. Gordon, 17
Flannery, Robert, 9
Fleary, Dinwall, 114
Flinchbaugh, David, 49
floods, 79, 110
F&M Schaefer Brewing Co. schooner, 134–35
Foley, Richard, 8
Folwer, Wendell, 124–25
Forehouse, Denny, 77
Forman, Tom, 126
Forse, Walter C., 16
Foster, John, 15
4-H baby beef title winner, 45
4-H parade, 77
Fox, Henry, Jr., 136
Franks family, 101
Freer, William, 16
Frenzel, Karen, 110
Frivolous Sal's Saloon, 136
Fulton, Joe, 25
Furnari, Peter C., 135

Gallagher, Betty, 23
Gallo, Dominic, 32
Gardner, Frank, 56
Gardner, Frank L., Sr., 17
Gardner Larkin, Margaret "Peggy," 43
Garno, Jack, 47
Garnot, Joseph, 15
Garrett and Ferris Garage, 75
Garrison, George, 127
Gennesee Trophy, 138
Gerdes, Margery, 16

Gershon, Norman, 91
Gibson, Barbara, 23
Gibson, Kathleen, 99
Gilbandt, Edna Best, 17
Gilbert, John, 20
Gilbert, Robert, Jr., 94–95
Gilbert, Steve, 20
Girl Scouts, 74
Girls' State program attendees, 125
Gleason, Jack, 138
Gleason, Joseph, 81
Goler, David, 24
Goler, Laura, 24
golf champion, 51
Gordon, Carol, 136
Gordon, Jim, 21
Gordon, Jimmy, 62
Graham, Martha and Lawrence, 63
Graham, Telford, 34
Grant, Joan, 41
Granter, Russell, 13
Gray, Joan, 43
Greco, Al, 29
Green Haven prison chapel, 126
Greenvale Farms, 41
Greenvale Riding Academy, 24
Gregory, Dick, 111
Greig, Robert G., 121
Greklek, Pancho, 132
Grey, Homer, 41
Grimm, Don, 72
Gromyko, Andrei, 90
Grote, Toni, 125

Hahn, Barbara, 61
Hahn, Jeanne, 61
Hahn, Johanne, 61
Haight, Charles, 10
Hajos, Louis B., 30
Hall, Richard, 51
Halloween party, 121
Hammond, Barbara, 24
Hammond, Jeanne, 24
Hannah, Dennis, 47
Hannan, John, 10
Harden, John W., 24
Harjes, George, 28
Harlem Valley basketball team, 20
harness racing, 70
Harper, Msgr. Francis, 99
Harriman, W. Averell, 87
Hart, James, 110
Hartzell, Andrew, 81
Hatfield, Ernest, 23
Hatfield, Ernest I., 90
Hawkes, Herbert, 13
Hayes, Roseann, 113
haywagon, 20
Healy, Joey, 57
Heaton, Jane, 43
Heilman, John R., Jr., 136
Helding, Barbara, 15
Hello, Dolly! (film), 133
Hemmindinger, Bernie, 50
Heppner, Ernest, 87
Heppner, Nancy Ruth, 87

Hewlett, Richard, 115
Hewlett, William, 115
Hicks, Mrs. Frederick, 132
Hirmberger, Richard Joseph, 75
Hoffman, Irving, 81
Hollman, Don, 30
Holzwarth, Jacob, Jr., 16
Holzwarth, Jake, 34
Hopeland Rest Camp, 57
Horn, R. J., 16
Horrocks, Ralph M., 9
Hotel Windsor fire, 33
Howard, Jim, 138
Howard, Mary, 135
Howe, William, 138
Hudson River, 13, 77, 92–93
Hudson River Day Line, 35, 43
Hudson Valley Philharmonic Orchestra, 127
Hunter, Al, 141
Hurd, Jerome, 75
Hyde Park Fire Department, 72
Hyman, Marilyn, 24

"I am an American" Day parade, 6–7
IBM, 59, 67, 95, 120
iceboating, 123
icebreaker at Mid-Hudson Bridge, 92–93
Idema, Joan, 43
Intercollegiate Regatta ticket, 15
Ironside, Alfred, 113
Istomin, Eugene, 127

Jackson, Dolores, 54
Jackson, Erwin, 30
Jackson, Mrs. John R., 54
Jackson, Kathy, 131
James Baird State Park, 99
Jewish Community Center campers, 24
John Maureen, Sister, 99
Johnson, Charles, 30
Johnson, Lady Bird, 118
Johnson, Mrs. Smith, 37
Johnson, Smith, 37
Johnson, Stanley, 50
Johnson, Walter, 67, 68
Jordan, Fritz, 34
Joseph, Barbara, 108
Joseph T. Tower Nurses Residence, 121
July 4th parade on Sheldon Drive, 72
Junior Chamber of Commerce, 60–61

Kahn, Sholom, 24
Kalliche, James, 69
Kalloch, Samuel J., 10, 64–65
Kallock, Elizabeth, 43
Kane, Charles, 123
Kane, Vincent, 105
Kaplan, George, 62
Kasica, Eleanor, 41
Kay, Meg, 100
Kearney, Grace, 41
Keenan, Pat, 57
Kefor, Marla, 77
Kefor, Tom, 77
Kehn, Donald, 55

Kelly, Gene, 133
Kelly, Miss S., 43
Kennedy, Barbara, 129
Kennedy, Betsy, 129
Kennedy, Carol, 129
Kennedy, Jack, 129
Kennedy, John F., 95, 109
Kennedy, Robert "Bobby," 95
Kenney, Pat, 73
Kent, Leaonard, 51
Key, Dick, 10
Key, Louis H., 24
Khruschev, Nikita, 90
Kilmer, Mal, 44
King, John D., 54
King, Martin Luther, Jr., 95
Kipp, Harold, 9
Kirchner, Carleton C., 28
Klump, Henry, 16
Knauss, Howard, 44
Knauss, Stephen, 129
Knickerbocker, Austin, 62
Kochis, Bob, 111
Kochis, Ronald, 111
Kogos, Eli, 24
Korean War, 59, 69
Kozlark, Robert, 43
Krieger Elementary School, 49
Krieger School, 43
Krom, Stephen, 94–95
Krulewitch, Melvin, 107
Kryhoski, Dick, 62
Kuhn, John J., 28
Kustas, Billy, 23
Kutz O'Shea, Nancy, 43

Laffey, Patricia, 43
LaGrange Town Hall, 128
Lahey, Barbara, 15
Laird, Robert, 34
Lake Walton Road (East Fishkill), 103
Landsman Kill Trail Association horse trails (Rhinebeck), 132
Larkin, Margaret "Peggy" Gardner, 43
Lasher, Fred, 130
Lasker, Mary, 118
Lazark, Joan, 24
Lear, Fred "King," 25
Leary, Jim, 136
Leary, Timothy, 95, 126
Lester, Florence, 50
Levine, Robert, 114
Lezon, Lois, 141
Licata, Frank, 105
Liffert, James, 55
Lindholm, Raymond, 43
Little Red Schoolhouse (Fishkill), 93
Lloyds family, 101
Lockhart, Michael, 116
Long, John K., Sr., 83
Long, Robert, 43
Lott, Richard, 81
Lovelace, Julie, 102
Lovelace, Louise, 26
Lovelace, Theodore, 26
Lovelace Mack, Linda, 82

Lovelace Mierzwa, Donna, 82
Lozier, George, 44
Luchton, Bernard, 16
Ludington's Mill (Putnam County), 97
Luesing, George, 56
Lupperalo, Barbara, 15
Lynch, Jean Marie, 79
Lyons, Jack, 20

MacArthur, Sheila, 130
Mack, Linda Lovelace, 82
Macky, Fred, 109
Madira, Tanny, 122
Magill, Bob, 21
Magill, Robert, 24
MaGuire, John, 104
Maile, Linda, 125
Main Street, Poughkeepsie, 71, 101
Majestic, George W., 107
Mallhouse, Raymond, 43
Malloy, Tom, 17
Manchester Road, 18–19
Mansfield, Joseph P., Jr., 88
Mansfield, Joseph P., Sr., 44
Mansfield, Marion D. Robinson, 44
Mantle, Mickey, 138
March of Dimes, 104
March on Washington, 95
Mardi Gras in Poughkeepsie, 60–61
Marino, Al, 10
Marl, Bud, 97
Marto, Richard, 109
Masch, Allan C., 83
Masch, Chris, 83
Masten, Timothy, 141
Masters, Francis R., 55
Mathews, Donald, 10
Mathis, Buster, 138
Matteson, Mrs. Harry D., 28
Mattiasich Schaefer, Irene, 51
Maurer, Theodore, 123
May, Herbie, 23
May, Rev. Arthur E., 24
McAllister, Robert, 34
McCabe, Frank Wells, 123
McCabe, Richard, 10
McCarthy, Joseph, 59
McCombs, Mike, 129
McCord, Bob, 72
McCord, Bobby, 53
McCord, Chester E., 53
McCord, Chester R., 53
McCord, Stella, 53
McCormack, Thomas, 59–60
McCourt, Barbara, 55
McCourt, Catherine, 43, 55
McCourt, Dorothy, 41
McDowell, Hugh, 27
McDowell, Vince, 27
McGaugrin, William, 81
McGinnis, Ann Marie, 139
McGinnis, Bernadette, 139
McGinnis, Timothy, 139
McGue, Dorothy "Dot," 73
McGuire, John, 9
McIssac, Harold, 34

McKenna, John, 137
McKiernan, Donald J., 130
McKinney, Jean, 15
McManus, Frank, 29
McManus, Frank J., 18
McManus, Patricia, 43
McNerney, Mary, 15
Melious, John, 132
Mellenthin, Herman, 21
Merrill Lynch, Pierce, Fenner and Smith office, 132
Mesier Park airplane crash (Wappingers Falls), 137
Messarad, F., 35
Metcalf, Harland, 61
Meyer, Richmond, 100
Michel, Catherine McCourt, 43
Mid-Hudson Bridge, 92–93
Mierzwa, Donna Lovelace, 82
Miles, Linda Dale, 108
Millbrook baseball team, 30
Millbrook Fire Department Carnival, 110
Millbrook Giants baseball team, 21
Millbrook hare-tracking event, 11
Miller, Al, 67
Miller, Bertha, 67
Miller, Fran, 67
Miller, Kenneth, 13
Miller, Mary, 67
Miller, William, 13, 121
Millerton High School, 10
Milrose Athletic Association, 50
Milrose Athletic Club, 50
Mima, Louise, 124–25
Minard, Raymond, 108
Mirto, Samuel, 9
Mitchell, Richard W., 122, 130
Mizerak, Steve, 122
Moehrke, William, 28
Moffit, Floyd, 68
Moltari, Rose, 62
Monell, Bobby, 104
Monell, Cathy, 89, 104
Monell, Robert W., 74, 79
Monell family Thanksgiving dinner, 85
Monteaux, Calude, 127
Montgomery, Robert, 69
moon landing celebration, 141
Moore, Sanford, 50
Morano, Ralph, 64
Morehead, Joan, 41
Morey, Mrs. C. Allerton, 12
Morgan, R. W., 24
Morgan, Relande, 15
Morse School, 86–87
Moses, Robert, 55
Mosher, Dale, 113
Moshier, Edward, 16
Mulford, Albert, 34
Murad, George, 34
Muraso, Louis, 68
Murphy, Barry, 50
Murphy, Margaret F., 70
Murphy, Marvin, 34
Murphy, Thomas W., 70
My Own Brucie (cocker spaniel), 21

Natoli, Joe, 138
Navy Day celebration, 46
Neal, Kenneth, 50
Neighborhood Youth Corps, 131, 132
Nejame, Charles, 28
Nelson House, 36–37
Neupauer, John, 50
Neuwirth, Ann, 20
Newman, Stanley, 24
Niagara Mohawk power station, 119
Nicholas, Chet, 21
Nicholl, Gay, 111
Nickerson, Cynthia, 10
Nicolik, Louis, 112
Niet, Johanna, 41
Noll, Chris W., 8, 13
Norrie Playground, 18
North, Howie, 44

Oakwood Friends School, 75
O'Donnell, Charles, 28
Oestrike, Richard W., 23
O'Hara, Mike, 50
Olah, William, 29
Olson, Raymond, 61
Orr, Libby, 17
O'Shea, Nancy Kutz, 43
Osoba, Francena, 125
Osterhoudt, Mary, 93
Ostrom, Billy, 90
Our Lady of Lourdes High School, 108
Overfield, Alfred, 72

Palmateer, George, 47, 51
Paquet, Paul, 81
Parker, Hardy, Jr., 97
Parker, Hardy, Sr., 97
Parker, Lula Mae, 97
Parker, Monique, 97
Parker, Renee, 97
Pasch, Lewis, 81
Pascoe, Ray, 34
Pasquazi, Thomas, 108
Passini, Matilda, 10
Patrice, Walter, 30
Patrice, Walter "Toot," 21
Paul Kefor's deli, 74
Pawling Rubber Co., 42
Peale, Norman Vincent, 37
Pearl Harbor attack, 7
Pemberton, John, 28
Perkins, Mrs. Donald, 113
Perlman, Murray A., 88
Perlmutter, Alvin, 23
Perlmutter Furniture store, 20
Persh, Mrs., 105
Peters, Francis, 134–35
Petrovits, Edgar M., 114
Phillips, Carmon, 50
Piggott, Bob, 47
Pimly, Harry, 27
Pittsburgh Pirates baseball school, 25
Place, James, 121
Pleasant Valley Aircraft Listening Post, 30
Pleasant Valley Elementary School, 124–25

143

Plover, Larry, 136
Polokoff, Shirley, 23
Post, Stanley, 29
Postoff, Lorraine, 24
Pottenburg, Betty, 45
Potter, Al, 21
Poughkeepsie Brown Derby basketball team, 22
Poughkeepsie Civic Ballet Co., 131
Poughkeepsie Civil Air Patrol, 55
Poughkeepsie Day School, 114
Poughkeepsie Fire Department, 8, 31, 96, 119
Poughkeepsie High School, 20, 72, 73
Poughkeepsie Journal building, 15
Poughkeepsie Little League Association, 122
Poughkeepsie Plaza, 59
Poughkeepsie Police Athletic League, 109
Poughkeepsie Police Department, 18, 38
Poughkeepsie Post Office ramp, 141
Poughkeepsie Railroad Station, 133
Poughkeepsie Recreation Commission, 61
Poughkeepsie Soapbox Derby, 53
Powell, Burr, 34
Prenting, Martha, 43
Presler, Edward, 54
Priddy, Alan, 16
Prince, Ken, 62

Qualls, John, 21
Quilla, Edward J., 128
Quinlan, Lawrence M. "Larry," 38, 129

railroad bridges, 13, 121
railroad gates, manual, 91
railroad stations, 79, 133
rainbow trout, 111
Ramsey, Alice Huyler, 123
Rappelyea, Kathleen, 10
Rauer, Kurt G., 90
Rawson, Constance, 49
Rawson, Terry, 43
Ray, Clayton, 72
Ray, David, 72
Raymond, Edgar, 28
Reed, James, 54
Reed, Leroy, 21
Reed, Morg, 21
Reed, Ross, 21
Reeves, Einar, 29
Remick, Jay Gould, 21
Repecki, Marlene, 15
reptiles day at school, 124–25
Reuter, Edmond J., 28
Reynolds, Allie, 119
Ribble, Michele, 131
Rideout, Arthur, 43
Riess, Frank, 113
Ringwood, Edward P., 70
Ringwood, Margaret Murphy, 70
Ritchel, Ken, 20
Ritter, Frank, 56
Ritter, Joseph, 17

Ritter, Leo, 17
Ritter, Louis, 56
Ritter, Sarah, 17
Roberts, Jessmine, 113
Roberts, Shirley Lee, 54
Robertson, Douglas, 43
Robertson, Grace, 35
Robertson, Neil K., 35
Robillard, George, 27
Robinson, Fred, 35
Robinson Mansfield, Marion D., 44
Rockefeller, Nelson A., 96, 128
Roe, Floyd C., 42
Roe, Leslie, 42
Roe Movers, 42
Rogers, Gordon, 43
Rolison, Jay P., 128, 132
Rombout Hunt Club (Beacon), 12, 100
Rombout School safety patrol, 113
Rood, Everett, 43
Roosa, Benjamin, 16
Roosevelt, Debra, 24
Roosevelt, Eleanor, 11, 47, 75, 90, 96, 104
  grave of, 118
Roosevelt, Franklin D., 7
  grave of, 41, 104, 118
Roosevelt Library, 118, 123
Rosenstein, Martha, 43
Ross, Ben, 34
Ross, Lanny, 12
Ross, Robert, 20
Rother, Jeanette, 10
Rowe, Arthur, 16
Rozell, Edwin H., 128
Rubin, Shirley, 21
Rucinski, John "Skip," 20
Ruehle, Mildred, 41
Ruggiero, Phil, 20
Russell, Charles, 43
Rutherford House, 16
Ryan, Joe, 72
Ryan, Margaret A., 28
Ryan, Marueen, 129
Rymph, George, 129

Sachs, Irma, 24
Sackelos, James, 106
Sackelos, Joseph, 106
Sackelos, Laura, 106
Sadowski, Paul, 50
Sagarin, Roy, 131, 132
sailing, 16, 134–35
Salt Point Fire Department, 76
Salvation Army gift-giving event, 140
Samuels, Paul, 16
Sarazen, Gene, 90
Sartori, Joanne, 125
Satz, Phyllis, 73
Scalzi, Mario, 72
Schaefer, Irene Mattiasich, 51
Schaefer, Robert, 20, 51
Schatz Federal Bearings Co., 26
Schermerhorn, Bill, 100
Schiller, Louis, 84
Schlichting, Margaret, 10
Schoentag, David C., 95

Schottler, Albert, Jr., 17
Schroeder, Creighton, 34
Schultz, Willard, 35
Scott, Bill, 44
Scott, Gerry, 44
Sculco, Donna, 109
Sculco, Frances, 102
Sculco, Frank, III, 102
Sculco, Jerry, 102, 109, 132
Sculco, John, 102
Sculco, Karen, 109
Seaboldt, Walter, 61
Secor, Robert, 28
Secore, Charles, 66, 70
Seeger, Pete, 59, 95
Segel, Elaine, 24
Seifts, David, 141
Seifts, Sharon, 141
Semmelhack, Richard J., 107
shad boning, art of, 108
Shepard, Martin I., 50
Sherman, Dale, 77
Sherman, Jimmy, 104
Sherow, Mrs. Allen V., 30
Sherow, Cecil, 114
Sherow, Mrs. Kenneth D., 30
Shorty, Bill, 77
Siber, Mrs. Carl, 96
Siebert, Kenneth, 113
Sift, William, 75
Siko, Irene, 10
Simmons, Keene, 62
Sims, Joseph, 21
Singer, Laurie, 135
Slutsky, Benjamin J., 96
Small, Henry, 129
Smith, Anita, 43
Smith, David, 41
Smith, Donald, 15
Smith, Jacqueline, 78
Smith, Malcolm, 16
snow equipment, 10, 11, 40
snowstorms, 102, 103, 140
Snyder, Linford, 28
Snyder, Robert, 28
soapbox racing, 53
Solotar, Jackie, 131
Somen, Shiela Whalen, 43
Sorensen, Theodore C., 135
Spackenkill Parent-Teacher Association, 104
Speedling, Shirley, 23
Spellman, Cardinal Francis, 63
Spiers, Ruth, 43
Spitz, Donald, 24
Spoor, Debby, 73
Spratt Park Pool, 10
Spross, Jane, 43
Sprout Lake children's camp, 52
square dancing, 12
SS *Vassar*, 37
St. Columbia School (Hopewell Junction), 125
St. Francis Hospital, 63
St. Francis Hospital School of Nursing, 41
St. Germain, Robert, 109

St. Joseph's School demolition, 116–17
St. Paul's Chapel (Green Haven prison), 126
St. Peter's Church, 88
St. Peter's School, 72, 99
Staatsburg Community Day celebrations, 87
Staffa, James Louis, Jr., 125
Staffa, Linda, 125
Stafford, William, 35
Stamm, Lawrence, 43
Stanford anniversary parade, 130
Steinberg, Florence, 23
Steiner, Charles, 67, 68
Steiner, William, 50
Stella, Joseph, 126
Stengel, Casey, 119
Stevenson, Wallace, 34
Stewart, John J., 61
Stewart, Kippy, 124–25
Stickles, Monty, 84
Stissing Mountain fire tower (Pine Plains), 131
stock car racing, 89
Stone, Mrs., 43
Storm, Janet, 49
Storms, Alfred E., 131
Stormville firehouse, 56
Streisand, Barbra, 133
Sturges, Peter, 50
Sullivan, John, 50
Sullivan, Paul O., 28
Superior Award of the Columbia Scholastic Press Association, 49
Susczynski, Frank, 101, 114
Susczynski, Irene, 114
Sutherland, Harold, 68
Svendsen, Penelope, 59–60
Swanson, Gloria, 23
Sweet, Elmas E., 69
Swift, Mrs. T.V.K., 44
swimmer awards, 129

Takacs, Larry, 50
Tarver, Marie, 136
Tarver, Rupert, 108
Teck, Michael, 50
television, educational, 86–87
Tellerday, Gerald, 110
Temple, Dean H., 17
10-mile race of YMCA, 50
tennis, 136
Terpening, Edwin, 44
Thanksgiving Day Parade, 64
Thomas, Alfred, 81
Thomas, Louis, 108
Thomas, Lowell, 37
Thomassen, Edmund, 8
Thompson, Janet, 8
Thorpe, Jim, 17
Tice, Ronald, 16
Tivoli High School, 50
Tomlins, Lois, 17
Tompkins, Bob "Jolly," 25
Tompkins, Charles, 16
Tompkins, Lewis, 16

Tom Thumb's wedding, 14–15
Town/Country Days farm tours, 94–95, 121
traffic lights, 120
train locomotive, 49
Traver, Charles, 102, 115
Trethewey, John, 67, 68
Triangle Service Station, 64
Tsitsera, Helen, 113
Tubbs, William W., 131
Turner, Joshua "Jot," 38
Twelfth Night carolers, 61

Underhill, Dorothea, 113
Underhill, Patricia, 49
Unger, Rabbi Jerome, 28
Union Street and Union Square demolition, 127

Van Benschoten, Mose, 97
Van De Bogart, Helen, 10
Vandemark, Roger, 28
Van De Water, John, 28
VanNosdall, Sally, 43
Van Nosdall, Shirley, 73
Van Tassell, James, 8
Varney, Richard, 115
Vassar Brothers Hospital laboratory, 113
Vassar College, 70, 80, 95, 111
Vassar College Alumnae House, 120, 123
Vassar Hospital 1,000th baby, 125
Vassar Hospital nurses residence, 121
Veeder, Gary, 35, 109
Veeder, Pam, 109
Verilli, Mrs. George, 132
Veterans Day services, 98–99, 105
victory celebrations, 36–37, 38–39
Victory Gardens, 32
Victory Lodge No. 1598 of the International Association of Machinists, 44
Vidal, Gore, 96
Vietnam Moratorium Day march, 140
Vietnam War, 95
Vincenti, Rudy, 132
Violet Elementary School, 58–59
Voerman, Gerald, 28
Von Duisburg, Albert, 38

Wallberg, John, 23
Wallwork, Joe, 72
Walsh, Mary Eileen, 41
Wanders, Joan Mae, 43
Wappinger Creek, 83, 110
Wappingers Central School, 16
Wappingers Falls Central School, 15
Wappingers Falls Main Street flood, 79
Wappingers High School, 47
Warring School, 23
Waryas, Victor C., 98–99, 119
Weigert, Lilli, 125
Wells, Elizabeth, 54
Wengen, David, 112

West, Cliff, 21
West, Cliff, Jr., 21
Western Publishing Co., 42, 67, 138
Westmoreland, W.C., 104
Westrum, Wes, 62
Whalen, Jack, 96
Whalen Somen, Shiela, 43
Wheeler, Gloria, 41
Whippo, Walter, 16
Whitaker, Burt, 44
Whitehead sand dock, 38
Whitely, William, 34
Whitesell, Alice, 10
Wigsten, Paul, 102
Wilbee, Jim, 16
Wilcox, Mrs. Frederick P., 121
Wilkie, Mrs. John, 44
Wilkinson, George, Jr., 16
William J. Long Co., 49
Williamson, Howie, 25
Willis, Don, 30
Willkie, Wendell L., 26
Wilser, Fred, 23
Wisserman, Barry, 120
Wisserman, Donald, 120
Wisserman, Donald, Jr., 120
Wisserman, Mary Lou, 120
Wisserman, Mrs. Donald, 120
Witek, Mickey, 62
Wohlfahrt, Fred, 51
Wolf, Charles, 126
Wollenhaupt, Arthur F., 128
Wood, Frank T., Jr., 24, 54
Wood, Jules, 21
Wood, Julius, 30
Woodruff, Rosemary, 126
Woodstock Music and Art Fair (Bethel), 95
World War II
  Community War Chest, 28
  Pleasant Valley Aircraft Listening Post, 30
  production for, 26
  rubber for war effort, 27
  sailors and soldiers, 9, 32
Wright & Wright garage, 88

Year of History Celebration, 90
YMCA, 17, 50
YMCA Y-Teens Club, 78

Zimmer, Ken, 10